"T.J.Cloutier is probably the premier tournament player in the world today."

—Doyle Brunson, Two-Time World Poker Champion

"Nobody knows how to win poker tournaments better than McEvoy"

—Russ Hamilton, 1994 World Champion of Poker

"Tom McEvoy's tournament advice is the best ever written."

—Barbara Enright, 1996 World Champion, Pot-Limit Hold'Em

"T.J. Cloutier is head-and-shoulders above anyone else...He is a legend...The greatest living no-limit hold'em player in the world."

—Mansour Matloubi, 1990 World Champion of Poker

"If there is one player that all of us fear the most at the final table, it is T.J. Cloutier."

—Berry Johnson, 1986 World Champion of Poker

"Tom McEvoy and T.J. Cloutier are an awesome team of hold'em players and writers."

—Phil Hellmuth, 1989 World Champion of Poker

ABOUT THE AUTHORS

World Series of Poker Champions Tom McEvoy and T.J. Cloutier are among the greatest tournament poker players today. They have won millions of dollars playing tournaments against the very best in the world.

McEvoy, the 1983 World Champion of Poker, has won four World Series titles. He is the author of the acclaimed *Championship Tournament Poker*, "one of the most important poker books of all time" according to Gamblers Book Club in Las Vegas, and co-author of ten other titles including *Championship No-Limit & Pot-Limit Hold'em*, *Championship Stud*, *Championship Omaha*, *The Championship Table*, *Championship Hold'em* and *No-Limit Texas Hold'em*.

T. J. Cloutier won the Player of the Year award in 1998 and 2002, and is considered by most pros to be the best tournament player in the world. He has appeared at the championship table at the World Series of Poker a remarkable four times, placing second in 1985 and in 2000. Overall, he has won more titles in no-limit and pot-limit hold'em than any other tournament player in the history of poker. Cloutier, who has won four World Series of Poker bracelets, is the co-author of *Championship Omaha*, *Championship Hold'em Tournament Hands* and *Championship Hold'em*.

CHAMPIONSHIP HOLD'EM TOURNAMENT HANDS

CHAMPIONSHIP HOLD'EM TOURNAMENT HANDS

Tom McEvoy & T.J. Cloutier

CARDOZA PUBLISHING

Cardoza Publishing is the world's foremost gaming and gambling publisher with a library of more than 100 up-to-date and easy-to-read books and strategies. These authoritative works are written by the top experts in their fields and, with more than 7,500,000 books in print, are the best-selling and most popular gaming books anywhere.

FIRST CARDOZA EDITION
Copyright ©2003, 2005 by Tom McEvoy, T.J. Cloutier, and Dana Smith
All Rights Reserved

Library of Congress Catalog No: 2004101419
ISBN: 1-58042-149-0

Visit our new website (www.cardozapub.com) or write us
for a full list of books, advanced and computer strategies.

CARDOZA PUBLISHING
PO Box 1500, Cooper Station, New York, NY 10276
Toll Free Phone (800) 577-WINS
email: cardozapub@aol.com
www.cardozapub.com

T

TABLE OF CONTENTS

TABLE OF CONTENTS

KEY CONCEPTS LEARNED AT THE WORLD SERIES OF POKER   245

TABLE OF CONTENTS

F

FOREWORD

by Dana Smith

This book will help you win limit and no-limit hold'em tournaments by taking you inside the heads of Tom McEvoy and T.J. Cloutier as they think their way through the correct strategy for playing limit and no-limit hold'em hands. We believe that by understanding the processes that champions use to win tournaments, you will have the edge on your competition.

Championship Tournament Practice Hands provides two types of instruction designed to help you become a better tournament player. First, the fifty-seven practice hands explain how champions use their skill and intuition to play strategically for maximum profit. Second, the forty-five key hands from the World Series of Poker demonstrate how world-class players have played in do-or-die situations. The authors' goal in giving you their analyses of these key hands is to help you gain useful insights into how tournament poker is played at the highest level.

These days, tournaments are harder than ever to win, partly because poker players have far more opportunities to practice tournament strategy than they had a decade ago. When I started compiling data on tournaments in 1990, Nevada casinos advertised thirty-five weekly low buy-in tournaments in a poker magazine. By 2003, that number had escalated to 110. Casinos in California, the poker capitol of the world, advertised 100 weekly tournaments in 1990 and 175 weekly events in 2003. Whereas only six other states advertised tournaments in 1994, card-rooms in thirteen other states advertised 125 weekly tournaments in 2003. Casinos also sponsored fifty-seven special events, many of them three-day tournaments with mid-level buy-ins.

Of course, you don't need to leave your living room to play a tournament these days. In 2003, for the first time in history, *Card Player* listed seventy weekly Internet tournaments (ten per day) sponsored by three poker sites. Add to these numbers the myriad small card-rooms that host tournaments but don't broadly advertise.

Big buy-in tournaments have proliferated

as well. Casinos across the nation advertised forty-eight major tournaments in 2002 with buy-ins from $500 to $10,000 that qualified players for points in *Card Player's* Player of the Year race, which T.J. Cloutier won in 1998 and 2002. With the advent of the World Poker Tour in 2002, $10,000 tournaments expanded to member casinos such as the Commerce Casino in Los Angeles, with the $25,000 buy-in championship event played at Bellagio in Las Vegas. No longer was the World Series of Poker the biggest game in town.

The fields in tournaments also have increased significantly. For example, 108 players entered the $10,000 championship event at the World Series of Poker in 1983, the year that Tom McEvoy won the title. In 1985, when T.J. Cloutier placed second in the title event, there were 140 entries. By 2000 when T.J. again finished second, the field had mushroomed to 512 entries, and in 2004, it was over 2,500!

Another reason why it's hard to win tournaments these days is because the level of expertise of tournament players has increased dramatically. When I asked Doyle Brunson whether the World Series was tougher to beat today, he said, "Oh, sure. The players are so good. I mean, those kids have learned all the tournament moves, they know how to play."

How did they learn to play so well so fast? Most of the young tournament players that I've interviewed over the years said they started playing low-limit tournaments for practice, read everything available on tournament strategy, observed how the masters of poker played the game, continually analyzed their own play, and then added their special touch as they graduated to higher levels.

The bottom line is this: the playing field is no longer even. Serious tournament poker players are putting more time, talent, and money at risk than ever before. Today you have to outplay smarter and more experienced players, including many professionals, in bigger fields with higher buy-ins.

Tom and T.J. want to help you move up the ladder. We sincerely believe that studying the way they think about how to play major hands in challenging situations will enable you to join them in the winners' circle far sooner than you ever imagined.

LIMIT HOLD'EM HANDS

I

INTRODUCTION

by Tom McEvoy

In this chapter, we'll show you the best way to play various types of hands in limit hold'em tournaments, particularly freeze-out tournaments that have structures similar to major, big buy-in events. We have depicted most of the practice hands as being unsuited because we want you to understand that the ranks of the cards you select to play are more important than whether they are suited. Some players use being suited as the reason to play certain hands when they should be looking more at its high-card value.

If poker were purely a game of skill, the best players would win all the time, but we all know that doesn't happen. Luck plays a greater role in tournaments than in side games because of the escalating limits and the rarity of getting premium starting hands in a compressed amount of time. The slower the limits go up, the more important tournament skills become. The faster the limits go up, the more significant the luck factor.

In tournaments with world-class fields of contestants whose skills are fairly equal, the player who catches the best cards that particular day and plays them well over time is the person most likely to win the tournament. Therefore, because so many world class players enter the major tournaments, no one has a huge edge over anyone else.

Players with lesser skills sometimes win tournaments or finish high in the money, and it happens often enough to keep them in the chase. Even in World Series of Poker events, I occasionally have seen mediocre players make it to the final table. But I have never seen an even remotely "weak" player win it all, no matter how lucky he was. And it doesn't happen often enough to discourage better players, because they know that skill will dominate luck in the long run. In fact, the more skill you have, the better chance you have to get lucky.

There is no magic formula for longevity in a tournament. All of the major tournament players that I have talked with about what happens when you get to that $150/$300 round or the $200/$400 round agree that you just have to catch hands at those betting levels. You can't manufacture a hand that doesn't exist. What you must do instead is play a patient, controlled game and give yourself a chance to get lucky. If you play too recklessly on marginal hands and get knocked out early, you can't make it to the higher levels where, if your hands hold up, you have a good chance of winning.

Although luck is always a factor in tournaments, it is your level of tournament skill that maximizes your opportunity to win. Much of this skill is knowing how to survive long enough to get lucky. The more correct decisions you make in the earlier rounds, the better your chances of surviving to the later rounds and getting a good rush of cards. Knowing how to make the most of the rush is what separates the very best players from the rest.

In *Championship Tournament Practice Hands*, T.J. and I will try to help you sharpen your skills in playing limit and no-limit hold'em, so that when the right cards start coming your way, you'll be there to catch them like lightning in a bottle.

BIG PAIRS

1. HOW TO PLAY ACES

THE BASICS

Suppose you're under the gun in a tournament and you look down at the boss hand, two aces. It doesn't matter what stage of the tournament you're playing or what your stack size is, you bring the pot in for a raise. In limit hold'em you don't limp in with two aces unless there is a maniac sitting behind you who raises every pot. In that case, since you know that he's going to raise the pot anyway, you might limp in and then put in the third bet after he raises. Whether you're in first, middle, or last position, raise with this hand. Don't give any free flops.

ACES IN A FRONT POSITION

A lot of people seem to think that slow-playing aces is a good idea. But suppose you have aces in first position, just limp in, and five other players also limp into the pot. Then the flop comes:

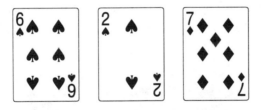

There's a pretty fair chance that someone has sevens and sixes, an open-end straight draw, a set, or a flush draw. If you had raised with your aces, you probably would have narrowed the field enough that you would only have had to beat one or two players and, if the flop came with raggedy cards, there would be a pretty good chance that you had the best hand.

The idea is to limit the field. You don't mind playing aces against one or two players, but you don't want to have to play against everybody. A pair of aces is the best hand that you can start with in limit hold'em, and you might as well try to win a pot without giving your opponents every reason to beat you. If the opponents who called your bet or raise before the flop are all regular players, lead at it on the flop unless big connected cards hit the board.

DANGEROUS FLOPS

A dangerous flop to your pair of aces is any three big connected cards. Say that you raised from a front position and an opponent reraised before the flop. The flop comes:

Or what if it comes K-Q-J, K-J-10, or Q-J-10? If you have put in at least three bets before the flop, you had better shut down. Don't lead at the pot because there is the possibility that a set, two pair, or a straight is out against you. If you're playing in a tournament, why should you risk losing a ton of irreplaceable chips with your aces? If somebody comes out betting at you, make up your mind right then whether you should play any further with your aces or throw them away.

If a pair is on board, especially a high pair, use caution in playing the hand because someone may have made trips. If you bet when there is a pair on board and get raised, slow down and reevaluate the situation before proceeding.

Now suppose you've raised before the flop with your pocket rockets, and the flop comes:

In this case, you probably would want to lead with your aces. Although a K-10 or 10-8 would give somebody a straight, players usually won't raise or call a raise with those types of hands. Of course, somebody could have flopped two pair, such as queens and jacks, but you can't be overly afraid of that.

OTHER TYPES OF FLOPS

Suppose you're holding pocket aces in a front position and the flop comes:

You can't give your opponents credit for flopping two pair or a set—there aren't that many two pair hands or sets flopped in poker. You have to be very aggressive, so lean at the pot. Now suppose the board comes with three cards of the same suit and you have the ace in that suit. This is another time when you should lead with your aces. Even if somebody has flopped a flush, you have a redraw to the nut flush. See how it gets played out. If you lead and it gets raised and reraised, you know that somebody probably already has a flush. In limit hold'em, you probably would continue with the hand to see at least one more card.

Of course, your ideal flop has an ace in it. If that happens, you just keep leading at the pot. Why would you miss a bet? But if no ace comes on the flop, you bet, an opponent calls, and an ace comes on the turn, should you go ahead and bet, or check in the hope that he will bet and give you a chance to check-raise him? You should bet. Don't try to set a trap by checking to him. If you check, he usually will as well. Then when you bet on the end, he may throw his hand away and you've lost one or two bets.

In summary, forget about limping with aces in the first scat. I've seen lots of players lose big pots because they limped with big pairs from up front and let somebody get into the pot with a 9-8 or 6-5. Then their opponent flops two pair or a straight and those aces are history. Don't give free cards.

ACES IN LATE POSITION

Now suppose you have a pair of aces in a later position. The people at your table are playing pretty decent poker, and somebody brings it in for a raise and another player reraises it. Should you reraise? Yes—put in the third raise. Don't think about trying to trap by just flat-calling, because sometimes when you try to trap you don't get the full value out of the hand that you should have gotten. So put in the third raise and hope that you get called by both of your opponents. You want to have the strength position. Remember that before the flop there's no such thing as the nuts, so if you get unlucky and lose the pot, so be it.

Suppose the flop comes:

One of your opponents leads at the pot. You hope he leads at you with his probable A-K. When he leads, raise him so that any of the little straggling hands that might have come into the pot will get out. You want to get it heads-up if you can. If he bets at you again on fourth street, just call. If he checks, bet. If the board rags off or pairs a little card on fifth street, raise if he bets into you — as long as no straight or flush card comes. If it does, you usually would call a single bet unless you know that your opponent would virtually never bet anything except a straight or a flush in this situation.

If the action is checked to you, you should generally check against tricky opponents and bet against timid or predictable players who don't usually check strong hands.

2. HOW TO PLAY KINGS

THE BASICS

The way that you play two kings in limit hold'em is pretty cut and dried. You treat kings the same way you treat aces, but you have to understand one thing about this hand: if an ace hits the board on the flop, you have to shut down.

If someone in an early position raises the pot and another player has called the raise, you must reraise with your two kings before the flop. You'd hate for one of them to have an A-4 and then see an ace hit the board on the flop. Make them pay you to get a chance at catching that kind of flop with their weak ace. Of course, there are some weak limit hold'em players who wouldn't lay down an ace-anything hand before the flop for all the tea in China. But even though you might lose to them now and then, these are the kinds of players that you want to play against.

You have to play it by feel. You must raise

with kings and if someone raises in front of you, it's a reraising hand. You want to get it heads-up. If you put in raise number two and your opponent puts in raise number three, you have to call him. There's a chance that you'll be up against aces, but not necessarily. Again, it gets down to watching your opponents. How aggressively they play two jacks or small pairs? Do they put in a third bet with two queens? Always be alert.

In summary, play two kings very aggressively before the flop and hope that an ace doesn't hit the board. Remember that when you're playing against only one or two players, a big pair has a good chance of holding up, but if you're playing against a big field in the hand, and all you have is one pair, you can't be nearly as aggressive. This is why you always raise with your kings to try to get it heads-up.

WHEN AN ACE HITS ON THE FLOP

Are there players at your table who will bet an underpair if an ace hits the board? If you check, will they bet with two jacks or two tens? Although this sometimes happens, they usually will have the ace if the pot has been raised before the flop. Know the people you're playing against and remember how they have been playing their hands.

Suppose the flop comes:

The first person to act comes out betting and the next player just calls. The action is up to you with one player left to act behind you. What do you do? Your kings aren't looking quite as good as they did before the flop, are they? In fact, they're looking a whole lot like losers! So you throw them in the muck.

Never be afraid to throw away two kings if an ace hits the board and someone bets into you or raises. You're a big dog to the hand, so you have to get away from it. After the flop, you have two outs twice, two more kings to hit on fourth street and fifth street. With an ace on board, what do you have?

After the flop you have to play the kings as the board dictates. You face the same types of danger flops with pocket kings that you face with pocket aces, only more so because of the danger of an ace flopping. You're starting with the second-best hand that you can be dealt, but when you have kings, it seems like every card left in the deck is an ace!

WHEN YOU FLOP A FLUSH DRAW

Suppose you have the K♠ K♥ and three spades come out on the flop:

Should you continue with the flush draw? Yes. You have second pair to the aces, and your kings beat the board's second pair (tens). You could also make the nut flush or three kings. Play this hand through the turn, unless the board pairs. Then you have to make a decision as to whether your draw is still alive. In a big action pot, a pair on the board can mean that a full house is out against you.

At the river it is a judgment call as to what you should do if you miss your flush and somebody bets into you. Try to get inside his head. Would he bet with a pair lower than aces or a lower flush draw than yours? If you think that he would, call the bet. But if you think that he has what he is representing—a flush or an ace—fold. And if there is another player still to act behind you, you should usually fold when someone bets into you.

3. HOW TO PLAY QUEENS

THE BASICS

In limit hold'em, two queens is a raising hand before the flop from any position, but is it a reraising hand? Sometimes, but not always. Remember that there are two overcards to the queen that people play all the time in limit hold'em. Suppose a solid player in seat one raises before the flop and another solid player calls the raise before it gets to you. One or the other of them might have two aces, two kings, or A-K. So you call with the queens, but don't reraise.

Now suppose that an opponent in the first seat has raised and a solid player in the second seat has reraised. You're in the third seat with a bunch of players to act behind you. What do you do now? Unless you're playing against maniacs, you throw your queens away. Although you've picked up a pretty nice hand, you don't have any money involved in the pot, and since it's been raised and reraised before you've even had a chance to act, it's easy to just throw them away in this spot. So what if the in the first seat only has two tens? The player next to him might have two aces, two kings, A-K, or even A-Q.

Let's say that you have pocket queens in the big blind. The pot has been raised and reraised and now it's up to you. You're already got a small bet into the pot, so you call. But if an ace or king comes on the flop, you're through with this hand. Of course, if a queen comes, you're in Fat City.

Now suppose once again that you are in the big blind with pocket queens and a player in late position raises with no more than two limpers already in the pot. In this case, reraising with your queens definitely is in order to try to narrow the field and get it heads-up if possible.

If a queen flops along with an ace or king (K-Q-6, for example), play it strong. Sets don't flop all that often, so don't be too afraid of someone having three kings. Against this type of flop, your opponents might put you on a king when you bet, and if one of them has an A-K, he's probably going to raise you. In that case don't reraise, but smooth-call the raise and then play for a raise or check-raise on the turn.

WHEN YOU FLOP AN OPEN-ENDED STRAIGHT DRAW OR OVERPAIR

Suppose you have raised the pot before the flop with pocket queens. The flop comes:

If you don't flop a queen, this is a good flop for your hand because it gives you an overpair and an open-ended straight draw. Just hope that you're not up against a K-Q.

Of course this would be a much better flop for you:

In this scenario you hope that your opponent has something like an A-J so that you can make a play with the queens.

People talk about getting two queens beaten all the time, but remember that it's still a very good hand. It's just that as you descend the ladder on the ranks of the pairs, you have to be more and more careful because the lower you go, the more overcards there are to contend with. Kings have aces as overcards, queens have aces and kings—and in a raised pot some of these cards are almost sure to be out. So, if the pot has been raised and reraised, there's a pretty good chance that even though you might have the best starting hand, somebody has one or two overcards ready to beat your queens.

Some players will raise with middle pairs of seven or higher. Say that an opponent raises with A-K, you call with two queens, and a player with two sevens also calls. He has two sevens to catch and the other player can land an ace and a king to beat you. But bear in mind that although you're less of a mathematical favorite versus two opponents, you're still the money favorite.

Remember that if you're playing in a ring game you can be a lot more aggressive with two queens than in a tournament. In tournaments, you sometimes simply have to get away from a hand. The good players get away from bad situations—they're not afraid to throw a hand away. Sometimes you even throw away a winner, but if you can't throw away a winner once in a while, you can't win at poker, because then you're just a calling station. I've never felt bad about throwing away a winner when I wasn't heavily involved in a pot. When I throw a hand away it is because I believe that the percentages are in *their* favor, not mine. The hand hasn't cost me that much—why should I give it a chance to cost me a ton of chips and find myself suddenly down to a short stack?

Now suppose the flop comes:

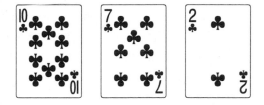

You have the Q♣. From there it's draw poker. You don't necessarily want to make the flush if someone is betting at you because he might have the A♣ or K♣, but there's a pretty good chance that you still have the best hand.

FLOPPING TOP SET ON A DANGEROUS BOARD

You have top set but there's also a straight possibility out there. What do you do? You still lead with your queens. If you get raised, you call the raise, but stop leading at the pot unless the board pairs. If a player bets in front of you, raise him on the flop. If you get reraised, just call and hope the board pairs. Unless one of your opponents raised before the flop, there is the distinct possibility that an A-K is not in play.

In this case, I would reraise, and if the guy who re-raised to begin with has A-K, more power to him—but you still have redraws to the boss hand. I don't suggest *not* betting the hand or *not* raising with it—why give your opponents a free card? If somebody has a king, 9, or 8, he can catch a middle-buster straight and beat you if you're just checking along and giving him a free card. For example, if a 9 comes on the turn, there are four cards to a straight on board and suddenly your set doesn't look too good with only one card to come. So, you have to lead with your queens—you can't allow everybody to get into the deck against you without having to pay for the privilege.

4. HOW TO PLAY JACKS

You can raise with jacks from any position when you are the first player in the pot. If you get reraised, just call—after you see the flop, you can decide whether to continue with the hand. Now suppose you're in late position and a couple of players have limped in front of you—you're still going to raise the pot, because you want to eliminate the blinds and everyone still to act behind you, if possible, and to build the pot. The value of your jacks is determined by the number of people playing in your game. The more players in the pot, even if an overcard does not flop, the more vulnerable you are. Heads-up, two jacks is a big-big hand.

If you're next to or on the button, you should raise with the jacks if the pot hasn't been raised yet. By raising you might knock out the people between you and the first bettor.

If someone reraises, you just smooth-call—if you get unlucky and an ace, king, or queen flops, you can always get rid of the hand.

Obviously if the flop comes jack-high, or has any jack in it at all, that's a big-big flop for you. But when it comes with overcards and you have two or more opponents, there's a pretty good chance that you're already beaten—and you're down to four outs, two outs twice.

WHEN YOU FLOP AN OPEN-ENDED STRAIGHT DRAW OR OVERPAIR

You have an overpair and an open-ended straight draw. This is not a bad flop to the hand but it isn't one that you can take to the bank either. Remember once again that limit hold'em is all about big cards—people call raises with Q-J in this game and if someone is in there with a Q-J, you're trying to catch a queen for a tie. As you get lower on the totem pole with your pair, other hands seem to be bigger in limit play (A-K, A-Q, even K-Q is only an 11 to 10 dog against two jacks). Two jacks just don't cut the mustard that well— you'll want to play against only one opponent and hope that you get a small flop or a jack.

Now look at this flop when you hold pocket jacks:

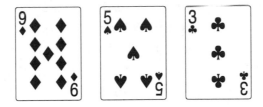

A broken board is a good flop for the jacks. Certainly someone could have a pocket pair to match the flop, but that could happen with any hand. In that case, the way your opponents play will dictate what you do with the jacks. You'll definitely bet if it's checked to you, and if somebody bets you might even put in one raise.

Raising on the flop in this scenario is a lot better than waiting until fourth street, because, in many cases, you can limit the field, which protects your overpair from draw-outs. For example, if a 10 comes on the turn, giving no straight or flush possibilities on the board, somebody might make two pair, tens and nines (people like to play the connectors in hold'em). Somebody holding cards such as Q-J also could have picked up a straight draw, but that's good for you. You like your opponents to pick up a draw with one card to come—if they get there, so be it, but you're a big favorite in the hand.

Late in a tournament the jacks are no better or worse than they are early on if you're playing at a full table. The limits are higher but the hand values remain the same any time that the table is full. A pair of jacks is a lot better hand shorthanded than it is in a full ring because you can be aggressive with them before the flop. For example, if you're at the final table with five players left, you can play the jacks a lot stronger than you could when the final table starts with nine or ten players. Just remember that if an ace, king, or queen hits the flop, your hand may be worth nothing.

BIG CONNECTORS

5. HOW TO PLAY A-K

"Big Slick"—that's what everybody in the rest of the world calls A-K, but in Texas it's called "Walking Back to Houston," because if you go to Dallas and play A-K enough times in no-limit hold'em and get yourself broke, you'll be walking all the way back home to Houston.

To be successful in tournaments, you have to win *with* an A-K and you have to win when you're *against* an A-K. In other words, you have to win the 11 to 10 situations.

In limit hold'em A-K is a big hand, a reraising hand, whether it's suited or not. Being suited just means it's a little more valuable, that's all. There's an old story about two guys who both held an A-K. The first one says, "Well, I have A♣ K♣ and you have A♥ K♠. I only need three cards in my suit to make a flush."

"Well, hell!" the second man answers. "I only need four cards in two suits—I have *two* flush draws against your one!"

In any position other than the small or big blind, you can reraise with A-K. And if you've been watching your opponents, you might even *reraise* against most of them. You can raise from the blinds but don't make a habit of reraising, because you will have to act first from the flop on, which puts you out of position. Always remember that A-K is a *positional* hand.

If you're around back and somebody has raised in front of you, reraise with an A-K because you have them on the defensive, and they will have to act first after the flop. If you're in the first three positions, bring it in for a raise. If you're in fourth, fifth, sixth, or seventh position, reraise with A-K. And again, if you're in the small or big blind, the most you should do is raise with the hand—do not reraise with it.

WHEN YOU FLOP TWO OVERCARDS

Suppose several people are in the pot and the flop comes something like:

You don't have any pairs, so you should check. A lot of people like to lead into the field with the A-K against this type of flop. Then they get played with, and almost invariably call the raise. Here's a typical scenario: Joe Blow bets it, somebody raises him, and he calls the raise because he has two big overcards. It rags on fourth street and Joe still doesn't have anything. He can't lead at it again but he calls when somebody else puts in a fourth-street bet—he's trying to catch that ace or king on fifth street because he's so accustomed to sucking out at the river. But the percentages are way against him.

Most of today's limit hold'em players play A-K—or ace-anything, really—like it's the Holy Grail. They raise it with A-Q, A-J, A-10—even with A-9 on down—because a lot of players love playing any suited ace. They like to raise with those hands, too. You're a big favorite over these types of hands with an A-K and that's why you always reraise with it *in position* (when you don't have to act first after the flop). Of course you also lose a lot of those pots when your opponents spike their only outs, but in the long run you're going to win a lot more than you lose because you started with the best hand.

T.J. was in the big blind holding A-K during a recent limit hold'em tournament with the limits at $2,000-$4,000. The first player raised, a reraise came from the number three position, and the player in fifth position called. What do you think T.J. did with the hand? He threw it away.

At least 80 percent of the time you should fold an A-K in this type of situation. All you have in the pot is your blind. It's going to cost you a double raise to see the flop when you might already be up against aces, kings, or even a suited A-K, which also would be a favorite over your hand. Furthermore, you're out of position on the hand.

DANGEROUS FLOPS

If you don't hit a pair to your A-K, any flop is dangerous! Suppose the board comes:

What do you do with Big Slick? Are you going to play it in the hope of catching a 10, ace, or king? A lot of players do, but we don't suggest it. Other than catching a 10, nothing else will make you the nuts. If you catch an ace or king, it could make a straight or two pair for somebody else. Of course, you might be up against a weak queen such as Q-7 suited—people play some strange hands in limit hold'em—and if you catch an ace or king on the turn, it would make you the boss. But for every time that you catch it, you'll miss it seven or eight times. Do you think that you could ever make enough money in the one pot where you catch to make up what you lost in all the other pots?

TRAPPING

In a tournament, the only time that you should ever trap is when you have the nuts, when you cannot be outdrawn. Say that you have A-K and the flop comes Q-J-10. Your opponent bets and you just flat-call because you've decided to trap him. Then the board pairs on the turn, and he bets again. Now you have to make up your mind how you want to play the hand. Are you going to raise him? Yes, give him one shot. But if he comes back over the top of you, all you have is a crying call at best (if you know that he can play at all).

6. HOW TO PLAY A-Q

An A-Q is a good hand in limit hold'em because so many people these days play small connectors and lesser holdings. You can raise with A-Q in from any position to limit the field, just as with A-K, but you don't usually want to reraise with it. If the flop comes ace-high or queen-high, you have a pretty good hand. When the flop comes queen high, you have top pair-top kicker; and when it comes ace-high you have top pair with second-best kicker. You would like to be up against a K-Q or Q-J when the flop comes queen-high because then you're sitting in clover.

There are a few situations, however, when you might reraise with A-Q in a tournament. Suppose you're sitting on the button and a player raises the pot with only enough chips for one more bet left in his stack. In this case, you're going to reraise to put him all in. By raising him all-in, you're not going to get blown out on the flop if it doesn't come with anything that helps you—and hopefully, you will knock him out. The reraise usually will knock the blinds out as well.

Another situation where you can reraise with A-Q is when you're in very late position and an aggressive player sits to your immediate right raises. You would reraise in this spot because you probably have the best hand, and you also have position on him.

Now take a look at this flop:

Oops! Suppose you're up against an A-K— now you're trapped. Although it's a very good hand in limit hold'em, you still don't want to put yourself in a bind with an A-Q. If your opponent is very aggressive on this flop, play it slow and just call. When you have an A-Q you usually would prefer the queen to hit the flop rather than the ace—except, of course, when your opponent has pocket kings.

Suppose the flop comes:

Although a lot of people play K-Q, you don't automatically put someone on it, so you can continue with the hand. If a king comes, you have the stone nuts, and an 8 gives you the second-best possible straight.

7. HOW TO PLAY A-J

An A-J is big trouble, and is played somewhat similarly to a K-Q. It's a little more attractive if it's suited, of course, but too many players overrate the value of suited cards. This is a hand that a lot of people play from almost any position—but if they play it from an early spot, they're making a mistake. You must have the right set of conditions to play an A-J, and if you are the first player to act in a full ring with aggressive players in it, this hand is a loser.

Remember that in tournaments, players are usually a little more solid than in ring games. This means that if anybody comes into the pot in front of you, or if it gets raised behind you, you probably are already beaten. Also, you probably are beat if someone brings it in for a raise in front of you, especially if a player sitting in the first two or three positions put in the raise. Or suppose you come in first and decide to bring it in for a raise and someone raises behind you—you probably are up against a better starting hand that has position on you.

There are times, however, when you might play an A-J very strongly. For example, if you are short-stacked you may commit to the hand, particularly if an action player raises from late position and you know that he has been bullying the table with a big stack of chips. If that is the case, you may reraise with A-J to get more money in before the flop with the intention of committing the rest of your stack after the flop.

You also might defend the big blind with A-J against a late position raiser. However if a solid player raises from very first position when you are in one of the blinds, you don't like this hand at all. What is he raising with? And what are you trying to make with this hand? The ideal flop is K-Q-10, but the chances of getting that flop are remote.

Suppose your opponent is drawing to a big pair and you flop an ace. He probably cannot give you any further action with the ace on the board. If you lead into him from the big blind, he probably will give up the hand if he's playing a big pocket pair, so you can't win any extra bets with the hand.

In another scenario, if he has a bigger ace than your A-J and you flop an ace, you're in trouble with a mediocre kicker. If he has raised with A-K or A-Q, you're going to get all the action you want and more. The only problem is that you're down to a three-out hand to hit your kicker, so you're in bad shape. These are the kinds of situations that we urge you to avoid as often as possible. This often means passing the hand or at least playing it very selectively. The time when you really like to play A-J is when you are in middle to late position and are the first to act.

Late in the tournament when you are nearing the payoff spots, A-J is a reasonably good hand to be aggressive with. It becomes more valuable to you, even in a full ring, because so many players are just trying to survive to come in the money. However, if there are a lot of big stacks at your table willing to mix it up, that's *not* the time for you to become aggressive with A-J. Of course if *you* are the one with the big stack against a lot of short ones, A-J is a good gambling hand in the very late stage of the tournament.

You have to use good judgment in playing this hand—you have to duck it when it might be a potential trap, and you have to play it aggressively when you think that you either can win the pot uncontested or when you believe that you have the nuts.

8. HOW TO PLAY K-Q

Limit hold'em is a big-card game—K-Q is a hand with two big cards. If the flop comes king-high or queen-high, you will have the second-best kicker at all times. And if the pot hasn't been raised, you can be fairly sure that an A-K or A-Q isn't out against you, so the K-Q ought to be the boss hand. It might come with both of them or it might even come A-J-10 or J-10-9, which would be terrific for your hand. As always, it matters whom you're playing against once the action starts after the flop.

When you're sitting in a middle position or later, you can raise before the flop with a K-Q. If no more than one player has limped in front of you, you can raise the pot—there's a good possibility that you have the best hand. If you raise before the flop and a player reraises behind you, you would call, particularly if the K-Q is suited. A lot of players reraise with jacks, tens, and nines, and if you have been observant and know you're dealing with someone who will raise with those types of hands, you're only an 11 to 10 underdog to catch one of your overcards, so you call the raise. If you don't flop to the hand, you can fold.

Now let's say that you limp in with K-Q and someone raises. You can call the single raise. Obviously, if an ace hits the board you're through with the hand. But if you're sitting in a late position and a solid player raises the pot in early position, you can just throw your hand away, since you have nothing invested in the pot. If you throw it away pre-flop every time you're in this situation, you'll be ahead of the game.

If you're in the big blind and the pot is raised in front of you, you can make the call for the single extra bet if you know that it cannot be reraised behind you.

Suppose the flop comes:

In an unraised pot you can be pretty certain that you have the best hand, and you have to lead with it. You want to prevent anybody playing low connectors from catching an inside straight card such as a 5, 4, or trey. And you don't want the board to pair either the 6 or the deuce on the turn, which can happen if you allow them to have a free card when they're sitting there with second or third pair. So you lead at it—if your opponents want to chase, let them do it. The idea is to get the most money you can, so you don't check these types of hands.

The worst time to check in poker is when you have a one-pair hand. There's a good chance that you could win the hand with a bet, but instead you checked, your opponents check behind you, and they all get a free card. Then they hit their second pair on the turn and you're in trouble. Some players check top pair because they don't want their opponents to know where they're at in the hand. They think it's good to be deceptive so that they can get them for the double bet on the turn. Wrong!

King-queen definitely is a playable hand in limit hold'em, but you have to be very careful with it because of aces. Any time you have raised before the flop with K-Q and one or more players have called the raise, you must be willing to release the hand if an ace hits on the flop. Suppose the flop comes:

Obviously, if it's an unraised pot, you have to call with your two pair if someone bets into you. But if the pot has been raised before the flop, you must be very careful. Make your best decision before you make the first call. If someone leads at it, you must be careful. Your two pair may not be any good, meaning that it's possible that you have only two outs.

For example, if an opponent has A-K or A-Q, you're playing to catch the opposite card, the only card that you have that is live. Or he might have J-10 for the straight. Actually, you have more outs drawing against the straight than you have drawing against A-K or A-Q. At least you have two kings and two queens to fill up.

If the flop comes K-Q-10 or K-Q-J and it's a raised pot, you also have to be very cautious. You have two pair, but in a raised pot there's a very good chance that you're up against a straight or a set on the flop.

Now look at this flop:

You bet your hand and get a couple of callers. Suppose the turn card is an ace: K-Q-6-A. Anybody who has a J-10 would have called your flop bet with the open-ended straight draw. Anybody who has an A-K will be there too. If the pot is unraised, you lead at it—your opponents will let you know where you stand. If the ace comes on fourth street in a raised pot, keep in mind that after calling a raise before the flop, a lot of players will also call a single bet on the flop with A-Q or A-6 hoping to make trips or two pair.

Of course you can't be afraid just because an ace hits on the turn. In loose games it isn't unusual for players to have hands like A-8 and call to see the turn card; then when the ace hits, they get aggressive with it. This is one more reason why you have to know your opponents.

In some cases when an ace hits the board on fourth street and somebody raises, you know that you're beat and you fold. But against players who like to play a lone ace, the raise is not as meaningful. When they hit that ace on fourth street, they think they have the best hand even though they have no kicker. If you understand the type of player you're against, you can make your best decision.

We can tell you a lot of things in these books, but you still have to develop and use insight about who is doing what when, and why. Know what's going on at your table at all times.

9. HOW TO PLAY Q-J

As we've said before, limit hold'em is a big-card game and queens and jacks obviously are big cards. But Q-J usually is a non-raising hand in most positions; it is a limping hand only. If the pot has been raised in front of you throw the hand away; if players have entered the pot in front of you, just call or fold. There are several scenarios in which you could flop a big hand to Q-J, but it's still not a raising hand. However, if everyone has passed to you and you're either the first one in or next to the button, you can consider raising against players who will often fold their blind hands.

Think of Q-J as two random cards, two random *big* cards, and play it that way.

Take a look at this flop:

In an unraised pot, if you hit either the queen or the jack on the flop you have a decent kicker, though not a great one. If the flop comes with a broken board such as the one pictured here, you can play it stronger than you could against a different type. If you bet on the flop and get raised, you have to make a decision as to whether you want to go any further. It is unlikely that the raiser would have two pair (J-4 or J-2) or an overpair (since the pot was not raised before the flop), but he may have a better kicker (A-J or K-J) or a set (if he limped into the pot with pocket fours or deuces). In many low-limit hold'em tournaments, people forget about the importance of a kicker when they flop top pair.

Now suppose you're playing in a multiway pot and the flop comes:

You have top two pair and obviously you're going to play the hand strongly. But suppose the board comes:

Anytime the flop comes with Q-J-10, K-Q-J, or A-Q-J you're in trouble. Even if it comes Q-10-8, there is a potential straight on board since some players like to play hands such as J♣ 9♣. If the board has straight potential, you have to be careful about how you play Q-J when you flop two pair.

MEDIUM CONNECTORS

10. HOW TO PLAY J-10

In the early days of poker there was a lot of conversation about J-10 suited being such a great hand. But so far in this book all of our big-card example diagrams are unsuited because we want to emphasize that you should put more value on the ranks of the cards than on their suits.

If a pot has been raised and called before it gets to you and you have a suited J-10, you are a definite dog in the hand—it being suited does not increase its value enough to warrant calling a raise cold. If the pot is raised and nobody else calls between you and the raiser, you still are a dog. Even if the raiser has only two deuces, you're only about even money with a J-10 offsuit. Not many people raise with pocket deuces, but the point is that against any underpair, you're only about an 11 to 10 dog.

The whole idea of poker is for you to have the best hand while your opponents are trying to draw out on you, not for you to have the worst hand trying to draw out on them. If you put your opponents in the bind of having to draw out to beat you, you always have the edge—you don't want to be the one who is going up against the edge. Remember this basic maxim of poker when you're playing hands such as J-10 and 10-9: If it's raised before you, you haven't lost a thing by not calling, and you will get two new cards the very next deal. So how hard is it to throw the hand away?

The myth that J-10 is such a strong hand is especially transparent when the pot has been raised. In a raised pot, you usually fold with J-10. A lot of players who believe that J-10 is a super hand, suited or unsuited, forget that even a lowly Q-6 offsuit has you beat.

If you flop either a jack or a 10 as top pair, you don't have much of a kicker, do you? The J-10 also can be a trap hand when you catch certain types of flops. For example, suppose you catch a 9-7-3 to it, which gives you two overcards and a middle-buster straight draw. A lot of players get themselves pot-stuck in this type of situation and wind up losing a lot of money to the hand.

The real strength of J-10 is the 10. A straight cannot be made without a 10 or a 5, so the strength of J-10 is the multitude of straights that can be made with it. You can flop a lot of different made straights to this hand, plus the straight draws that you can flop to it.

The J-10 is a hand to be played, yes, but it is one that you must play very carefully under the right conditions. You don't want to give it too much credit because it has definite liabilities. Some of the right conditions for playing the hand are multiway, unraised pots when you are in late position, or when you are defending the big blind for a single bet.

Obviously if you flop jacks and tens, you have a pretty good hand, but what if you have called a raise before the flop with J-10 and the boards comes:

Now what are you going to do? Or suppose the flop comes A-Q-5. Sometimes you can take off a card to make the inside straight, but the chances of hitting those middle busters are slim. Also, you must not call a bet in these situations if players can raise behind you.

Although you seldom raise with J-10 before the flop, it still is a hand that is a part of the big-card family, as is any hand with two cards 10 or higher. If someone raises in front of you, don't cold-call the raise with J-10 (although a lot of players do, because you know that you have the worst of it—and who wants that?

This is a hand to play when the pot has *not* been raised and you are in late position. If you limp in, you can call a single raise and take a flop to the hand. But here's the key to playing J-10: If you don't flop to it, get rid of it immediately. You don't want to get involved in a situation where you flop a jack or a 10, an overcard is on the board, and you continue with the hand—this can cost you a lot of money.

If you flop good to it, that's another story. You may flop a straight, three jacks, or three tens. Even the K-Q-4 flop might be okay, in which case you can take one card off. We don't suggest continuing with the draw if you don't hit it on fourth street—why pay a double bet for the draw? However, the pot odds come into play in this situation. Even though you don't usually like to play drawing hands in tournaments, you might continue if the pot odds are good enough.

Suppose you have the J♠ 10♠ and the flop comes:

You have an open-ended straight draw and a three-flush to go with your J♠ 10♠. In this case you can draw to the hand. Let's say that you don't make the straight on fourth street but you pick up a flush draw to go with it—the board now reads:

In this case, you can continue with the hand. But if you make a pair on fourth street against the K-Q-4 flop, you have a big decision to make. Say that the turn card is a jack and the board now reads:

Obviously the jack might have made a straight for someone else, while you have bottom pair and a four-straight. Someone else could already have an A-10 or a 10-9, and at the most you would be drawing for a tie.

Now suppose it is late in the tournament — it's down to two shorthanded tables. At this stage hands like K-Q, Q-J and J-10 increase in value. The discussion so far applies to full-ring action, but as the tables get shorter these big-card hands increase in value. When you're playing nine-handed at a table, eighteen cards have been dealt. When you're playing five-handed, only ten cards have been dealt, moving your high cards up the ladder.

Just remember that you want to flop something nice to the J-10, and you don't want to put yourself in a position where you can get killed with it. In tournaments this is the type of hand that can cost you all of your money. Let's say you call a bet before the flop, you might even call a raise before the flop and you flop some possibilities. So you call another bet on the flop, you don't make it on fourth street, and now you have to decide whether to continue.

Your thinking goes something like this: "Well, I've already lost two bets before the flop and a bet on the flop. Now it's going to cost me a double bet on the turn. Should I pay for it or not?" Then you rationalize, "Hey, I've got so much money in the pot already, I'm gonna continue." That's bad poker. Take your loss and move on to the next hand.

Now suppose the action is multiway and the pot is huge. You'll probably take the card off and go on to fifth street with the hand because you have the possibility of winning a big-big pot, and, because the action is multiway, you have proper pot odds. But if you're playing heads-up or against only two opponents, the odds are so against your making the hand that chasing the money in the pot just isn't reasonable.

Multiway pots tend to come up earlier in the tournament when you're gambling at a lower level, and very seldom do you see multiway pots in the late rounds. This is a factor to take into consideration with drawing hands—and J-10 is a drawing hand from the get-go. You don't have much to start with, you only have a jack-high hand, and any overcard is a favorite over the J-10. Enough said?

11. HOW TO PLAY 10-9

If you are in late position with a lot of chips, and several players have limped into the pot, 10-9 might be worth calling with. If you catch a good flop, you may be able to take somebody off with the hand. But it isn't a raising hand, suited or unsuited. 10-9 is a very tenuous hand, just two cards that you might draw to once in a while from late position to see what happens.

Of course, you also can play it from the

blinds in unraised pots. When it costs you only half a bet extra in the small blind or nothing at all in the big blind, it can be a very nice hand because there are a lot of flops that will help it—but there also are a lot of flops that can hurt it.

Say that someone raised the pot before the flop and you called the raise with 10-9 on the button. The flop comes:

Because the pot was raised before the flop, aces, kings, queens, or jacks could be out against you. Also, A-10, K-10, Q-10, and J-10 all have you beat. You have flopped top pair, but you have no kicker. Always remember that a kicker is a big item in hold'em. "When I first started playing," T.J. admitted, "I thought that when I had any ace, I really had a hand but all I had was a loser. It took me all of a week to learn that kickers are important."

12. HOW TO PLAY 8-7

If you have a lot of chips or a medium stack and your hand is only 8 high, it's a chip burner. Even if you're playing an 8-7 against a short stack, there's a pretty good chance that he can beat an 8-high hand, so you're taking the worst of it. Instead of breaking your opponent, you're giving him a chance to double up.

There are very few conditions in which you can play a hand like 8-7 suited in a tournament: you can use it in the small blind for an extra half-bet in an unraised pot; in the big blind for a single raise if you have a lot of chips and it's multiway action; or on the button for one bet when several limpers already are in the pot.

The 8-7 suited is virtually unplayable in early to middle position. If you're in late position and a few limpers are in the pot, that's a different story—now you have position. You need to have at least two callers in front of you to play the hand, even when you're next to or on the button. If you get a good flop, obviously you can play it further.

But you have to get a perfect flop to a hand that's only 8 high, otherwise it just eats up your chips. For that reason, it just isn't a hand that you usually want to play in a tournament. What you really want to play in tournament poker are the ones that you *don't* have to get a perfect flop to—which is a big difference between tournament and ring-game play. You don't want to have to take any heat with this type of hand. This principle also applies to other suited connectors such as 7-6 and 9-8.

However if you are extremely short-stacked and have a chance to enter a multiway pot, you might call a raise with the 8♣ 7♣ and even put in the rest of your chips with it, but only because you're in bad shape anyway. Also, it is unlikely that other people are playing the same kinds of cards in a raised pot, so your hand might be live. You are playing for the added value that comes with a multiway pot; in other words, if you are extremely short-stacked, you might gamble with this hand if you can get a good price.

Some players don't mind taking a shot at the blinds with middle connectors like 8-7 when they're in late position and are the first one in the pot, especially if the blinds are either exceptionally conservative or running desperately low on chips. They rationalize playing this kind of hand by thinking, "I've got some chips and I have a chance to break this guy." We do not recommend this type of play, and here's why.

Suppose you're playing $300-$600 late in the tournament and you have $5,000 in chips. If you raise in the late stages with hands like 8-7 suited, you're burning up your chips, and if you do that two or three times, you might find yourself suddenly down from $5,000 to $3,000. "I wonder where my chips went?" you ask. "I haven't made any bad plays." But you have, so let your opponents make those kinds of plays, not you.

It isn't your job to knock people out of the tournament. You only have to knock one player out—the last one. To expand this concept, imagine a player has J-2 in the big blind in a limit hold'em tournament. The blinds are $1,000-$2,000 and somebody who only has $4,000 in chips pushes all of them to the center in an all-in raise. Everybody passes to the big blind and he says to himself, "It's only gonna cost me $2,000 more, so I'm gonna call and try to bust him." This is one of the worst plays in tournament hold'em. It isn't your job to break him. It isn't your job to lose an extra $2,000 on a hand that you had no business playing in the first place, yet you see so many players doing it.

When you are tempted to play those kinds of hands, always ask yourself, "Do I want to put my money in with the best hand, or do I want to have to draw out to win the hand?" That $2,000 might be worth $8,000 in a later hand when you have good cards with three callers in the pot with you. But if you lose that $2,000 you don't have it to win their $6,000. And that can make the difference when you get deep into the tournament.

MEDIUM PAIRS

13. HOW TO PLAY TENS

When we talk about big pairs, we mean aces, kings, queens, and jacks; medium pairs are tens, nines, and eights; and small pairs are deuces through sevens. Of course, there isn't a big difference between eights and sevens, but, all the same, the bigger the pair the better off you are.

Two jacks is what we consider to be the median hand in limit hold'em; that is, it's about even money whether one or more overcards flop. But with two tens, you're the "favorite" to see one or more overcards hit the board. This doesn't mean that you should not play pocket tens just because you're afraid of the flop—two tens actually is a very playable hand in a lot of situations. But it isn't playable at all in others—for example, when it's been bet, raised, and reraised before the flop by solid players sitting in early positions. In this scenario, generally consider passing pocket tens unless everybody comes into the pot and you get a huge price (knowing that you probably would need to flop a set).

The only advantage that two tens have over some of the other pairs is that you always need a 10 or a 5 to make a straight, and with 10-10 in your hand you have a little more straight potential. In our opinion, two tens have the best chance of holding up against one or, at most, two opponents. If the pot is played multiway, you almost always have to flop a set or make a lucky straight to win.

If you are in early position, you usually can bring it in for a raise, and when you are the first one in the pot from middle position on, you *always* bring it in for a raise (and in this case, we do mean always). Remember that after three or four people in front of you have passed, it's an automatic raise.

If one or two guys limped into the pot,

it's usually best to just flat-call to try to see the flop cheaply. If you are playing in a super loose game where everybody sees a lot of hands before the flop—especially in the early stages of a re-buy tournament (during the re-buy period) when most people at your table are doing a lot of pre-flop gambling—you may just limp in from early position with pocket tens in order to mix up your play a little bit in the hope of flopping a set. You are not limping to slow-play the hand—two tens is not a big enough hand to slow-play—rather, you limp in because you expect to get multiway action anyway, and because players at these loose tables don't respect early-position raises during the first rounds of the tournament. Realize that if you raise and get four or five callers, you probably will have to flop a set, so you might as well see the flop cheaply.

But that no longer is the case from middle position on. When several people already have passed, it isn't shaping up to be a multiway pot like it could be if you just limped in from early position. So, when three or four people already have passed and there's nobody in yet, you want to put as much pressure on the pot as you can before the flop. Players will know that they're not getting a price on their hands. A lot of times, people will play a hand that they think they're getting a price on that they won't play in a much shorter field. You are trying to narrow the field by getting players to lay down hands such as A-3 suited.

If it's a freeze-out tournament and everybody plays a bit more conservatively in the early stages, which usually is the case in tournaments with no re-buys, you usually will bring it in for a raise.

If you are in late position and someone sitting to your right in middle to late position is the first one in the pot and brings it in for a raise, you generally want to reraise to try to isolate him and get the action heads-up. Your equity goes up if you can drive everybody else out of the pot. You probably have the best starting hand, and you will have position on the raiser. If he reraises, just flat-call and make a decision after you see the flop. Obviously, if you flop a 10 you have a powerful hand. Your main concern then becomes deciding how to extract the most money you can from your opponent. Usually the later the position that the initial raise comes from, the less strength the raiser needs to bring it in for a raise.

A lot of people in that position raise with hands like pocket eights, nines, A-8 suited, or two high cards such as a K-J or Q-J. If somebody at your table has those cards, your pockets tens are a slight favorite, and you have superior position. If two overcards to your pair come on the flop, you can get away from the hand cheaply. Of course the raiser might have a big pocket pair—there are no guarantees in tournament poker. You just have to make the best decisions possible—which you're rewarded for in the long run.

14. HOW TO PLAY NINES

Two nines is a very tricky hand to play up front. It's a little too good to throw away, but it's also very vulnerable in an early position. Nines, tens, and jacks are in about the same category. A pair of jacks is about 50-50 to catch one or more overcards on the flop, and, of course, a pair of nines is weaker than that. In early position you might just limp in with the nines because you want to see the flop cheaply.

Suppose you're on the button with pocket nines and one or two people have limped into the pot. You usually would just call, because if you raise the limpers probably are going to call the single raise—and the types of hands that they limp with are often the connecting cards such as Q-J or J-10, all overcards to your nines. It is possible that you might force out the blinds with a raise, but that's not certain to work.

Now here's the case for raising: Two nines is a hand that is past the "halfway point" (a pair of eights) and, of course, is better than all lower pairs. You know that you're probably starting with the best hand and it only costs you one extra bet to raise. You also know that most or all the limpers are going to call you. You're building the pot and hoping to win a decent haul with the nines, realizing that you can get away from them if overcards hit the board on the flop. In that case, the limpers will often check to the raiser, giving you a chance at a free card by also checking. Nothing says that you have to play the hand past the flop if it comes with overcards.

You must be smart enough to get away from the nines. A cardinal sin of poker is to bet after everyone's checked to you when the flop comes with two or more overcards. Why not take the free card? Because if you bet and are check-raised, you're in trouble — you have to give up the hand immediately and wind up losing a bet when it didn't have to cost you anything to see the turn card. But with just one overcard on board, you can bet if it is checked to you.

In tournaments, the number of players at your table affects your play. Raising out of the big blind with two or three limpers in the pot is something that you would not do in a full ring—you would rather see the flop cheaply with several limpers already in the pot. But if five players or less are at your table, you're in the big blind and somebody has limped in before you, you would raise with those two nines because you probably have the best hand. And if the table is shorthanded, you might even raise from first position.

When you have 9-9 in middle to late position and three or four people have passed, making you the first player in the pot, you might bring it in for a raise unless you have a strong feeling that someone is ready to tramp on you with a reraise. When you are on or next to the button with only one weak limper in the pot, you want to raise to get heads-up against one opponent.

Here's another scenario: You're playing at a high level in the tournament and you're on the button with two nines. Two limpers have entered the pot in front of you. There's a good chance you might just throw the nines away. You're thinking, "We're playing at a high level and I don't want to risk $3,000 on this hand if overcards pop out on the flop. I just have a feeling about this hand." So you chuck them in the muck. Any time that you throw away a decent pair, remember that although you didn't make money on the hand, it didn't cost you anything either.

15. HOW TO PLAY EIGHTS AND SEVENS

If the pot is raised and reraised before the action gets to you, pocket sevens or eights usually are not hands that you want to play unless five or more have called. If the pot will be played with a big field, you don't mind gambling with the middle pairs in the hope of flopping a set, especially if you are short-stacked. In that event, you might even cap it with your case chips since you are getting four or five to one on your money. Naturally this means that you are in late position with the sevens or eights, because otherwise you can't be sure that the pot will be played multiway.

With your case chips in the pot, even

if overcards come on the flop, you will at least get to see all five community cards and hope to get lucky. You aren't capping the pot because you think that 7-7 or 8-8 is the best hand against four or five opponents before the flop—you're capping it because you're getting a good price for the hand and you're in bad shape anyway. You're willing to gamble, hoping to get lucky and get back in the tournament. Even if you lose, what have you lost? You were short-stacked anyway, so you really haven't lost that much.

So, there are times when you can be aggressive with pocket sevens or eights and take your chances with them—namely, from late position or sometimes from middle position. If you are up against fairly conservative players and no one has entered the pot, you can bring it in for a raise from late position. Raising from a middle position is a little more dangerous, as there are still several people to act.

If you are playing at a fairly loose table, it's a marginal decision as to whether to bring it in for a raise. The tighter the table, the more likely you are to raise. If you are the first one in from a later position you can almost always bring it in for raise because two eights figures to be the best hand most of the time.

Suppose you have pocket eights. Your best scenario is flopping a set. The next best flop would give you an overpair with a straight possibility. However, when you have an open-ended straight possibility to go with your overpair of eights, the flop comes 7-6-5, for example, someone else may have an even better hand, a made straight, for instance. Even so, you can be fairly aggressive with the hand to the river.

When you flop an overpair with pocket eights (or lower pairs) *without* an open-ended straight possibility, it's dangerous when the flop comes coordinated. For example, suppose the flop comes:

5-4-3 or 7-6-4 are connecting boards that can give someone a straight on the flop, a straight draw, or possibly two pair. So, even when you flop an overpair with your pocket eights, you have to use caution and judgment in how you play the hand, particularly if someone has shown a lot of pre-flop strength. In that case, you may be up against a larger overpair. For example, say that you're in late position with pocket eights and decide to call a raise by a solid player. If the flop comes something like 7-4-2, you might think that you have the best hand, but in fact you may be up against a pair higher than your eights. As always you have to play the player as well as the hand.

If the action is checked to you after the flop, you are going to fire a bet at the pot, especially if your eights are an overpair to the flop. Even if there is an overcard to your pair on the flop, you can bet aggressively so long as you think that you have the best hand. For example, suppose only the blinds have defended your late position raise and the flop comes:

With only one overcard, you can consider it a favorable flop and bet if it's checked to you. If you get check-raised, you will have to make a decision as to whether your opponent is check-raising with a jack or a better hand than yours, or whether he is check-raising with two big overcards, or even a seven. In other words, is he raising because he has a hand, or because he thinks that the flop missed yours?

Now suppose the flop comes:

How do you like this flop? You like it, but it's still dangerous. Anyone playing a Q-9 has a made straight and anyone with K-Q has a premium straight draw. You can continue to play your set aggressively until you have reason to believe that someone has a better hand than your trips. If another straight card comes on the turn and there are two or three other people in the pot, most of the time you should shut down. You don't necessarily fold because the pot is usually big enough by then to give you proper odds to try to fill up. If someone bets into you, just flat call.

Of course there's another danger to consider: If the board pairs with a jack or a 10 and someone is playing a J-10, his full house is bigger than yours. If it is checked to you, you can bet. If someone bets into you, you can put in one raise. Then if you get reraised, just flat-call. In other words, you may lose a few bets to this hand but you won't lose the maximum with your lower full house.

If a fourth straight card comes on the turn and a very tight player who has called the betting on the flop fires a bet at the pot, you probably should give him credit for the straight. You can call his bet on fourth street in the hope of filling up on the river, but if you miss you probably should fold your trips. That is a very delicate laydown, especially in tournaments when people are not making a lot of plays at the pots. Against the "new breed" of overly aggressive player, you might consider calling even though you don't like your hand that much.

SMALL PAIRS

16. HOW TO PLAY SIXES

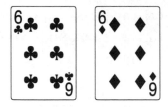

When you play a pair of sixes or lower, you virtually always see overcards on the flop, so you almost never have an overpair to the flop unless it comes something like 4-4-2. And when overcards don't flop, a straight possibility usually will be out there. Sometimes you even will have a straight draw yourself with the sixes.

As with medium or small connectors, if you play these small pairs (fours, fives, and sixes) from early position, you obviously are very vulnerable. These are not hands that you want to take a lot of heat with.

You can play small pairs from late position for the minimum bet when there are several callers in front of you. If you limp with a small pair and someone raises behind you, go ahead and call one more bet. But if it gets raised and reraised behind you, the proper play is to fold, unless you get multiway action from four or more players, in which case it is okay to call the double bet in the hope of flopping a set and winning a monster pot. The hand can be quite deceptive if you flop a set to it, and if that happens you can win more money with it than with connectors because the set is better disguised.

If you are on or next to the button and are the first one in the pot, you might take a shot and raise with two sixes. You will weaken the value of your hand by just limping, so either fold or raise. You have the semblance of a hand against two players (the blinds), or at least one of them (the big blind), so you can raise with the sixes. You're hoping to win it right there, or at least get heads-up with the big blind when you have position on him and hold what probably is the best hand.

Always remember that you have to fold small pairs out of position. Any time you come into a pot from the first five seats in limit hold'em, you had better be able to stand a raise, otherwise you have made a bad play. Yet you see people playing small pairs all the time from an early position. If someone brings it in for a raise in front of them, they routinely call. Their thinking is that the raiser probably has A-K whereas they already have a pair and can flop a set to it. They forget about all those pairs that are higher than theirs, or that their opponent might hit the ace or king.

These types of people play "optimistic" poker rather than optimal poker. But it's not optimism that will help you win at the tables — rather it's playing the game correctly. And playing the game right says that playing little pairs up front spells t-r-o-u-b-l-e.

Keep in mind that limit hold'em is a big-card game. If you play sixes, fives, fours, treys, or deuces from early position, you're just asking to get beat and lose your money. You absolutely have to hit a set or get some other fantastic flop to win with these little pairs. So, the best formula for playing sixes or lower in the first three or four seats is to think of them as though they were a 3-2 — throw them away. Even though you might put your opponent on overcards only, you should still pass these types of hands.

Remember that people play a lot more hands in ring games because the pots are multiway far more often than they are in tournaments, especially in California where it isn't unusual to see five or more people in each hand in ring games. They're hoping to hit a set playing small pairs in ring games, and there's nothing wrong with that. Just don't do it in a tournament because small pairs usually burn up your money.

17. HOW TO PLAY FIVES

Although a pair of fives is a small pair, it has an added value: You need a 5 or 10 to make a straight and you have two of those cards in your hand. So, it can be pretty sweet if you catch a flop such as 4-3-2, which gives you an open-ended straight draw and an overpair. Sometimes you can trap someone who has an ace in his hand, and if you're lucky to catch an ace on the board you've beaten him with your straight. Of course it's a little bit dangerous if a 5 hits the turn because then you have a set but the ace has made the straight. When that happens, your set may trail on the turn but still you don't necessarily have to give it up, just play it with caution.

A good flop to your pair of fives is something like:

In this case, two fives could easily be the best hand, and even if they aren't you have a lot of potential to improve to the best hand. Sometimes just hitting the third 5 (which also is the inside straight card) will give you the best hand.

Of course, two fives is vulnerable to overcards, so any time that two face cards hit the board you're done with the hand. An exception to this rule of thumb occurs when you're playing against one conservative opponent and he has checked to you. In this case, you might fire a bet at the pot, especially if you have made a late-position raise with your fives pre-flop. The late position raise is a move that you can make if you're on or next to the button and nobody has entered the pot.

Now suppose the flop comes:

Your conservative opponent checks to you. In this case you might bet your two fives because there is a good chance that you have the best hand. If your opponent calls, you can reevaluate on the turn. If he is the kind of player that you think he is, he isn't calling because he has a weak jack. He's probably calling with overcards. If a blank comes on the turn and he checks again, you can bet your pair again, and if he check-raises, you can reconsider your play again. The more conservative he is, the more credit you can give him for having a real hand — if he's so conservative would he really check-raise you if he didn't have a better hand? It's a judgment call, and you're playing both the cards and your opponent.

As with all pairs, no matter what their rank, flopping a matching card to your fives is what you're hoping for. Sets will win 80 percent or more of the time when you flop one.

Playing fives in early to middle position when you're the first one in the pot usually isn't the right thing to do, especially in tournament play, because you can't be sure that you'll get a good enough price for your hand, and because you're out of position, and as a result, very vulnerable. For the most part, then, fold pocket fives out of position unless you're playing in the early stage of a re-buy tournament in which a lot of people are gambling. In that case, you might limp in and hope that you flop a set.

In freeze-out tournaments, pocket fives are a pass from early to middle position. If you're sitting in the cutoff seat or on the button and you're the first one in the pot, you can bring it in for a raise, especially against players who are not liberal blind defenders. If two limpers already are in the pot, you can call a single bet from late position.

If only one limper is in the pot, pocket fives is a pretty marginal hand—unless the limper is very short-stacked and you have a lot of chips. If you are the one who only has a few chips left and he has a lot, you might decide to take a stand with your fives. Or if both you and the limper are very short-stacked, you might play your fives. In any other situation when there is only one limper in the pot, you are better off to pass pocket fives.

18. HOW TO PLAY FOURS

If you're getting three or four callers in a raised pot and you're sitting around back with a lot of chips, obviously it's nice to have pocket fours. But playing heads-up or even a three-way pot isn't a good idea with little pairs.

From a front position, I throw pocket fours away as though it's 7-2. You can only stand a raise with pocket fours if you're getting very good pot odds, and obviously you're hoping to flop a set and rake in a good pot. But if you don't flop a set to your little pair there are very few scenarios where you can play them. In other words, you need to get very lucky to win with small pairs.

Small pairs are takeoff hands in no-limit when you have a lot of chips. Keep in mind that 4-4 is only an 11 to 10 favorite over a 6-5. When you take that into account, there are a lot of hands better than two fours. Pocket fives have a little more value because 5 is a straight card.

Yet time and time again you see players strapped for chips and clinging to life play these hands: One player has $3,000 in chips, looks down at a baby pair, and moves in everything he's got. If he gets called at most he's an 11 to 10 favorite but he could also be a 4.5 to 1 dog. Of course, if you're anteing more than $200 or so, and you have $800 with the blinds coming up, that's a different situation. In that scenario, you might play the hand, but with $3,000 or $4,000 in chips, you have time to wait for a better hand.

While there are certain situations when you can play small pocket pairs, you should usually avoid them. If you stand a little raise in no-limit with a baby pair, it's almost always because you have huge implied odds, lots more chips than the other players, and you're getting multiway action, whereas playing hands like 4-4 heads-up for a raise is almost always a mistake. People who move in with these types of hands are just asking to get broke.

POT-LIMIT NOTES

It's better to play small pairs in pot-limit than in no-limit. You might play a small pair from early position in pot-limit, and you may even stand a small raise with it—so long as you are in decent chip position. The basic difference is that in pot-limit you usually don't have to put as much money in the pot to see a flop as you do in no-limit. Obviously, if you call a raise and get reraised you can always fold without losing too many chips. Do not call raises very often with little pairs in pot-limit or you'll do big damage to your stack. Pick your spots and your opponents carefully.

19. HOW TO PLAY TWOS

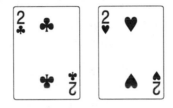

You have to be very selective about the situations in which you play pocket deuces. You don't want to play two deuces from early position if you're the first one in the pot, and if you are in middle position, you don't want to get involved unless two or more limpers already are in the pot. However, if you are playing a re-buy tournament in the early stage (during the re-buy period), when a lot of people are playing each pot, you might possibly play pocket deuces from up front—but that's the exception, not the rule. In a normal freeze-out event, you must be very careful with them.

You can sometimes call a raise with pocket twos when you're in late position and know that you're going to get five-or six-way action. For example, suppose a couple of players limp in, another player raises, and one or two people behind him call the raise cold. In this scenario you don't mind gambling if you're in the cutoff seat or on the button, and you can call the raise in the hope of flopping a set.

There are times when you can raise with pocket deuces, but only when you are the first one in the pot and you're sitting in the cutoff seat or on the button, or when you are in the small blind versus only the big blind—and only against blinds who are not extremely loose players. In this case, there's a good chance that two deuces is the best starting hand, although they're still very vulnerable to overcards.

In tournament play, we use deuces as an example of the smallest pair possible and talk about raising with them as a semi-bluff, and so on. But late in the tournament when people are just hanging on, trying to survive to the money table, you can raise with *any* hand—it doesn't need to be as "strong" as two deuces.

If you are the big blind, you might call a single raise with pocket deuces, and if you're in the small blind, you might see the flop for a half a bet. Usually you want to have two or more people already in the pot. After the flop, you follow the "No set, no bet" philosophy and dump the hand, the same as you do with other small pairs.

Suppose you flop a flush draw with your small pair. Drawing to a flush is something that you don't usually consider doing because a higher flush card can so easily beat you—unless you're heads-up against a very aggressive player. If you are in that situation and make the baby flush on fourth street, you might want to call him down if he bets, especially if he's the type of player who will represent a lot of hands. (You certainly can't do that against two or more players because one of them usually will have you beaten.) Suppose your aggressive opponent checks to you and you bet your little flush. You probably will only get called if you arc beaten, so you just check it down rather than value-bet your hand.

SMALL CONNECTORS

20. HOW TO PLAY 5-4

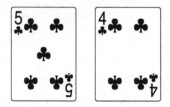

The small suited connectors, of course, are not as strong as the middle suited connectors because many times they make the weak end of the straight. If you have a 5-4 suited the only time that you have the nuts is when A-2-3, 2-3-6, or 3-6-7 comes. If it comes 8-7-6 you can be in a world of hurt with the idiot end of the straight because a lot of players like to play 10-9. So, the higher your connectors, the better off you are. It goes without saying (but

I'll say it anyway) that if the hand is suited there is no guarantee that you'll make the best flush with it. A flush is *not* what you're hoping to make with a hand like this.

Suppose you flop a flush. Any player who has a single higher card in your suit can make a bigger flush on the turn or river if a fourth suited card hits the board. Most players who flop a four-flush with a suited overcard in their hand will take a card off to see fourth street at least. If the fourth flush card comes on fourth street, you have to be very careful in deciding whether to continue with the hand.

You can play this type of hand when you are in the small blind and it costs you only half-a-bet more to see the flop. You also might defend the big blind with small connectors in a multiway pot. Or you may play it on the button or in very late position provided there are at least two other people already in the pot *and* you don't think that someone will raise behind you.

This is where the "Two-Limper Rule" discussed in *Tournament Poker* comes into effect. The rule states that when two or more players have entered the pot for the minimum bet, a multiway pot is developing. In that case, you will get a nice price to also limp in with suited connectors, small pairs, and other hands that require multiple callers in order to turn a profit. However if you sense that there are too many people yet to act behind you, any one of whom is likely to raise the pot, pass the hand.

There are some special situations that dictate that you can raise with this type of hand. Suppose it's late in the tournament, you are in late position with a decent amount of chips, and you know that the other players at your table are just trying to hang on for a payout. In these situations it doesn't matter so much what your cards are—with two suited connecting cards you at least can make a straight or a flush with the right flop and ambush the opposition.

This play is one type of semi-bluff. You have three ways to win: Your opponents surrender without a contest; you out-flop them if they call the raise; or you could win with a bet on the flop and your opponent folds because he missed. It's pretty sweet when you've raised the pot with 5-4 from a late position, get there with it, and trap someone with a better hand. T.J. tried this play in a hold'em tournament when he was the first one to enter the pot and raised on the button with 5-4. The big blind flat-called the raise with a pair of jacks, and the flop came A-5-5. Needless to say, T.J. took the pot.

BIG-LITTLE SUITED

21. HOW TO PLAY A-7

An ace suited or offsuit with a card lower than a 10 is what we call an "any-ace" hand. In loose ring games you'll see a lot of people playing "any-ace," particularly if the ace is suited. Then when they come into a tournament they play with that same mentality, particularly during the first three levels of the event. These types of players play very aggressive poker, usually overbetting their hands and giving a lot of loose action. They are the maniacs, the ones who rule the early stages of tournament play—but they aren't around later

Any-ace suited is a weak hand, although there are situations when it is playable. You can call with it from the small blind for half a bet in an unraised pot. From the big blind you might call a single raise from a late-position raiser who you know could be out of line. You may also call with this hand when you're on or next to the button in an unraised pot with several limpers already in. In this case you figure that the ace might be good because if someone else had a big ace, he probably would have raised. And if everyone has passed to you on the button, it's probably correct to raise with an any-ace hand to attack the blinds.

Just remember that if several people have limped into the pot and you call on the button with A♦ 7♦, the flop that you're looking for is three diamonds or aces-up. You're not looking to win with a lone ace—if you happen to win with the ace by itself, that's just a bonus. So when you put your money in the pot, you're looking for two sevens, an ace and a 7, or three diamonds on the flop.

Suppose you're in the pot with a suited A-7 on the button when three or four players have limped in front of you and the flop comes with an ace. If everyone checks to you, there's a good chance that no one else has an ace (or they would have bet it), so you can bet the hand and see what develops. If you get check-raised, you can reevaluate.

You have to avoid problem hands in tournament poker, and the best way to do that is simply to *not* play them. Certainly avoid playing hands like A♦ 7♦ from the first three or four spots in front of the big blind. Get rid of it so that you can avoid having to make a lot of tricky decisions later in the hand.

Actually A♦ 2♦ through A♦ 5♦ is a better hand than A♦ 7♦ in a multiway pot because you can make straights as well as nut flushes with wheel-type aces. Having a 5 along with the ace gives you a straight card for either the wheel or a low straight. If you're going to play an ace with a suited wheel card, play it in the same situations that we have outlined above—calling a half-bet from the small blind, defending the big blind from a late-position raiser, and limping in late position.

However, if that late-position raiser is the guy with a layer of dust on his chips, it isn't worth trying "to keep him honest." You know that either you're a dog with your ace or you have only one overcard. Remember too that you're taking the worst of it trying to hit your suit to win.

Suppose you're sitting in the big blind with the A♥ 5♥ in an unraised pot and the flop comes:

You have top pair with a weak kicker and a three-flush, but poor position. If you're in a multiway pot, you should check and see what develops. If you are up against just one or two other players, you can bet the hand; if you get played with, reevaluate your strategy after you see the turn card. Sometimes you bet again, sometimes not. It's a judgment call based on your evaluation of your opponents and the texture of the board.

If you hit your kicker on the turn, bet again, and if you're raised, go ahead and flat-call. Don't forget that a card that makes your hand stronger also could strengthen your opponent's hand. In this example, when you hit your kicker (the 5) and make two pair, one of your opponents could have made a straight if he had an 8-7 in his hand. You also could be up against a bigger two pair or even trips. It is doubtful that either of your opponents holds an A-K because there was no pre-flop raise.

22. HOW TO PLAY K-5

Time and time again you'll see people play big-small suited cards in tournaments—Q♣ 7♣, J♥ 8♥, all those hands. And you'll even see players occasionally win with them—but over time these types of hands will burn up all their chips. So, let *them* play them, but not *you*. A king suited to any small card that is not a connecting card is a bad-news hand. What do you do if you flop a king? You have no kicker.

There are certain situations, however, when you can play a big-small suited hand. You can play K♣ 5♣ in the big blind in an unraised pot, and you might play it in the small blind for a half-bet. Also, if you are in the big blind and a player has raised all-in, you might call the raise with a king-small suited to try to beat him *if* no one else has called.

Another scenario in which you might

consider playing the K♠ 5♠ type of hand is when you're in late position against very conservative players, especially when they're trying to hang on for the money late in the tournament. In that case you might make a raise that is based more on position than on the strength of your hand—you're just trying to muscle them. Of course you can do that with any two cards—the hand itself might have no value (it could be 3-2 offsuit) because all you're trying to do is steal the blinds.

Although some players routinely play hands like J♦ 7♦ on the button, we do not advise it. When you are tempted to play big-small suited cards on the button, remember what we have emphasized: If nobody has a hand in front of you, there still are two players sitting behind you (the small and big blinds) who might have a real hand. And if one of them does wake up with a hand, you have put yourself in harm's way.

With a king-, queen-, or jack-small hand, you usually will be drawing to the second, third, or fourth-nut flush if two suited cards come on the flop. When you play the A♠ 5♠ your premium hand is the nut flush. With the K♠ 5♠, your premium hand is a high flush, but you could make it and still lose to the ace-high flush. Although the chances that you're up against the ace-high flush are slight, it does happen. And when it does, it can cost you a ton of chips. In addition to having no kicker, the inferior flush draw is why big-small cards are trouble hands.

ONE-GAP HANDS

23. HOW TO PLAY Q-10

Q-10 is a hand that requires a lot of judgment to play successfully and profitably. Being suited always makes a hand more valuable, of course, but suited or not, Q-10 is a tricky hand. Half of the battle in limit hold'em tournaments is avoiding difficult situations—you don't want to feel like it's a crap shoot when you look at your hands. This is why Q-10 should usually be played from late position in unraised pots rather than from early position.

From early position, you pass this trouble hand. In a raised pot, the hand loses a lot of its value, which is one reason why it is awkward to play from an early position. Suppose you call with Q-10 and the action is raised behind you. If you flop a pair to the hand, you cannot know for certain whether you have the best kicker. This makes it a particularly dangerous hand to play in a raised pot. Many people play Q-Q, Q-J, K-Q, A-Q, so when you flop a queen to your Q-10 you're out of position, stuck with a big kicker problem, and in a world of hurt. Therefore it's a big losing hand from early position, especially in tournament play because you can't afford to bleed away your precious chips on this type of hand.

Even from middle position, the hand usually is unplayable, but there's always an exception, of course. If you're in the re-buy period of a tournament and people are gambling, you might try to see the flop cheaply with this hand if you're prepared to mix it up and buy back in. If the Q-10 is suited and there are one or two limpers in the pot, you have more reason to see the flop with the hand. Offsuit the hand is, at best, a marginal call and you must play very cautiously after the flop unless you flop a lucky straight.

In late position, from the cutoff seat or the

button, you might raise with Q-10 if you're the first one in the pot to try to get heads-up with the blinds. If there is only one limper in the pot and you don't think that he is slow-playing a monster hand, you might call from late position with Q-10 but you generally wouldn't raise.

A dangerous flop would be something like Q-J-4, an extremely perilous board. You've flopped top pair with a weak kicker and if you hit the 10 on the turn, it could make someone a straight. Someone may already have queens and jacks or even a set of fours. Essentially, you're looking to flop two pair, or a lucky straight. If you flop trips, you might be in kicker trouble, although you're still going to take your chances with the hand. You'd much rather hit a 10 than a queen, of course. You may flop to the hand and still have to fold on the flop. The Q-J-4 flop is a good example. If it's bet and raised before it gets to you, you don't have a hand and you simply must fold.

Basically with Q-10 you're looking to flop a straight, two pair, trips, or flop top pair and have everybody check to you so that you can take the lead and feel reasonably comfortable. Of course, if you are check-raised you can't feel comfortable with it at all.

24. HOW TO PLAY 10-8

This hand is playable under very limited conditions. You can play it from the small blind for one half-bet in an unraised pot. You also can play 10-8 from the big blind for a single raise if five or six players are in the pot and there is no possibility that someone will reraise, in which case you're getting a good price for the hand. You might also play 10-8 on the button in an unraised pot. But coming in cold for a raise when you are not in the blinds is something that you should not do with 10-8, particularly if there is any pre-flop heat.

Naturally 9-7-6 is a great flop to the hand; other good flops include J-9-7. However if someone has a Q-10, he most likely will draw to his open-ended straight, and if he hits either a king or an 8 you probably will lose a few bets to the hand. That is the danger in playing hands like 10-8—you might find yourself up against a higher straight on the turn or river, even if you flop the nuts.

Dangerous flops occur when you flop top

pair with your weak kicker and someone bets very aggressively, especially if the flop has connecting cards.

Suppose the flop comes:

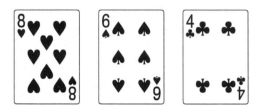

A lot of players these days play hands like A-8 or K-8 suited, and some play one-gap connectors such as 7-5. You could easily be up against a higher pair, a made straight, or two pair on the flop. When you flop top pair with a 10, the 8 is a very weak kicker. Anyone playing an A-10, K-10, Q-10, J-10, or 10-9 has you beat. So you must be very careful when you play a 10-8.

25. HOW TO PLAY 9-7

You must be selective and cautious about the conditions under which you play 9-7 suited. Although being suited is always preferable to being unsuited, that alone is not enough reason to play the hand.

In the small blind, you can call one half-bet with 9-7 if the pot has not been raised. Or, if the pot has been raised and there are five or six people still in, you might gamble and call the bet from the small blind to see the flop. In the big blind you can call a single raise when there are three or four people in the pot. If you're up against one early-position raiser, you should pass from both the small and big blinds. You need a little bit of a price to play this hand—you don't want to go up against an early-position raiser with a hand that is only 9 high. If you are in middle to late position in an unraised pot, there should be at least two limpers already in the pot. Occasionally, you can raise with 9-7 when you are the first one in the pot and you have the cutoff seat or on the button. Your intention is to take a shot at the blinds if they are conservative players.

A great flop to the hand, of course, is 8-6-5, in which case you make the nut straight. You also make a straight with a J-10-8 flop, but it's still a dangerous situation. Someone playing a Q-9 has the nut straight and anyone playing K-Q is going to be drawing to an ace or 9 to make an even higher straight. As with the 10-8, you can flop a straight with 9-7 and still not end up with the nut straight.

If you flop a flush to your 9-7 suited, obviously you have a huge hand, unless you're up against a bigger flush. You can play this aggressively and hope that another card in your suit does not come on the board, and that the board does not pair. If it does happen you must let the betting dictate what further action you take. This is where your powers of observation are tested: Will your opponent have the nerve to represent a high flush? Will he represent a full house if the board pairs? You have to make the tough decisions—nothing in this case is cut and dried.

26. HOW TO PLAY 7-5

Now let's take a look at hands such as 7♣ 5♥, middle connectors with one gap (9-7, 8-6, 7-5). When can you play these types of hands?

Suppose you're playing the opening round of a re-buy tournament, at the $15-$30 level. Five limpers are in the hand for $15 each, and you are on the button. With all those limpers in the hand, it may be worth your while to put in the $15. If you don't flop to the hand, you can fold it. But you also might get a big flop to it and make a lot of money on the hand. In any other scenario, the hand is worthless.

TWO-GAP HANDS

27. HOW TO PLAY K-10

You have to be very selective about how you play a K-10. This hand can spell trouble any time that you play it in a raised pot. In tournament play, K-10 is a reasonable hand with which to attack the blinds (if they are conservative players) when you're in late position and are the first one in the pot. In fact, when you sit on the button or two spots in front of it, you should think about raising to try to steal the blinds with any two cards 10 or higher when you are the first one in the pot.

Against a solid player who raises from up front, you fold a K-10 even if you are in the big blind and no one else has called the raise. If several people have called the raise, you might consider playing the hand if it is suited, although you generally are better off ducking this hand against an early-position raiser. Ask yourself this: "If Solid Sam has raised from early position and several people have called him, what could they be calling with?" They could easily have K-Q, A-10, K-J, or better.

In that case, if you don't catch a lucky straight or two pair to your K-10, you probably are beaten. This isn't a hand that you can take a lot of heat with. However if an action player raises from a late position, particularly the button and you are in the big blind with K-10, you generally would call to see the flop.

If you're in the small blind heads-up against the big blind, you can raise with K-10. If one limper is in the pot and you're in the small blind you can see the flop for one half-bet. From late position with one or more limpers in the pot, you might consider limping in for the minimum bet.

The hand has more value if the pot has not been raised. What do people normally raise with? Big cards. Therefore, the hand has more value in late position in an unraised pot. Because people limp in with hands such as K-Q, K-J and A-10, you still have to be cautious even if you flop top pair. If someone fires a bet from early position into a field of four or five people, you don't like your hand that much because there's a good chance that someone has a better kicker.

28. HOW TO PLAY Q-9, J-8

You prefer playing this type of two-gap hand against a single opponent. If you do play this type of hand in a multiway pot, the fact that both cards are of the same suit helps, but your flush possibilities could get you in trouble because of the possibility that someone else is holding a bigger flush draw.

You play a hand like Q♥ 9♥ more for its rank and connectedness than you do for the flush potential. With this sort of hand in a multiway pot, you don't even necessarily *want* to make a flush. Any time you play a suited hand that doesn't have the ace in it, you're using it for its straight value or possibly to make two pair or trips. Making top pair usually isn't enough to take the pot.

The value in a hand like this rises in certain circumstances. Suppose somebody raises with A-Q and nobody calls the raise. You're sitting in the big blind with Q-9 suited and decide to call. The board comes Q-9-rag, and just like that, you've trapped the A-Q.

The times that you play these types of hands are:

(1) When you're in the small blind for half a bet.
(2) When you're in the big blind for a single extra bet.
(3) When you're in late position in a multiway pot, preferably an unraised one.

You do not initiate the action with this kind of hand unless it's blind-against-blind. Or, possibly, when it has been passed to you on the button and you can attack the two blinds. Other than these two situations, you don't initiate the action yourself with hands such as Q♥ 9♥.

This is not a hand that you can take a lot of heat with, but I've seen people fall in love with this kind of holding. Any suited two-gapper must be played under the right set of conditions, thoughtfully and cautiously. Certainly these are not hands that you play in the first two or three positions in front of the big blind—the only suited two-gapper that can be played from early position is A-J.

29. HOW TO PLAY 10-7

You might play a mid-rank, two-gap hand suited or unsuited from the small or big blind for half a bet in an unraised pot from the small blind, but if the pot has been raised, you should surrender it from both the big and the small blind positions

Getting trapped with these hands is your biggest fear. Invariably you flop either a 10 or a 7 for top pair and become involved. You've caught a little piece of the flop and often, you die with it. Always be leery of "free" hands.

DEFENDING THE BLIND WITH INFERIOR HANDS

Tournament poker players lose a huge amount of chips when they defend their blinds with hands that they would not have played if they were in a different position. Too often they call with a substandard hand, catch a piece of the flop out of position, and wind up losing a lot of extra bets with a hand that they shouldn't have played to start with. All of these types of hands are big-big trap hands.

Suppose a player raises all-in with $2,000. You're in the big blind and have $10,000. A lot of players think that the big blind has to call the raiser, but he doesn't. Calling a raise in situations like this is one of the worst moves that you can make in tournament poker. Although you want to break your opponent, you don't want to lose a lot of chips trying to do it. Why would you want to double up an opponent by playing a bad hand?

But if he has $2,000 and you have $30,000 it's worth taking a chance to knock him out of the tournament. In this situation you can take a shot at breaking the guy because the worst that can happen if he wins the hand is that he will have $4,000 and you will have $28,000. But when you have only $10,000 and he has $2,000, he will double up to $4,000 if he wins the hand and you will be down to $8,000. Now how do you like it? You have allowed him to get up off the carpet. I can't tell you how many times I've seen someone play a sub-par hand because he thought that it was mandatory to call, lose the hand, double up his opponent, and then see that same player came back to haunt him later in the tournament.

30. HOW TO PLAY 8-5

Being suited is always preferable to being unsuited when you play a two-gap hand. But even when they are suited, you usually must have exactly the right set of circumstances before you can play these types of cards. It's difficult to make the absolute nuts with these hands—even when a two-gap hand makes a straight, it's sometimes possible for someone to make an even higher one. If the hand is suited, you prefer to make a straight rather than a flush because of the chances that someone will make a better flush. If that happens, you probably will lose a few bets to the hand.

Generally speaking, you won't play these hands at all but, as always, there are a few exceptions. One of them is when you are in the big blind and your two-gapper is suited. In this case, you can call a single raise if several people already are in the pot. Whether the hand is suited or not, you can play it for one-half bet from the small blind when several players already are in the pot. If you don't flop to the hand, it's very easy to get away from it.

If you catch a little piece of the flop, proceed with caution. Even if you flop top pair, the hand is vulnerable, especially with several people still in, because your kicker is bad. You would like to have a straight possibility to go with your pair, which would make your hand stronger. If you flop two pair or a straight, of course you can be aggressive with the hand.

With any two cards you can attack the blinds from a late position when it is late in the tournament and everyone plays super-tight, just trying to make it into the money. As a result you can attack with hands like 9-6 and 8-5 when you are the first one into the pot, because it doesn't matter what your cards are—they could be 7-2 offsuit. You're not raising on the strength of your hand, you're just making a play at the pot to steal the blinds when you think that everyone has tightened up their game.

Sometimes you even get a lucky flop to your hand, which is a bonus. Occasionally you're going to hit something. Generally speaking, however, these are "trash hands" that require exactly the right circumstances to play, which usually means playing them for one half-bet from the small blind or for the minimum bet from the big blind.

THREE-GAP HANDS

31. HOW TO PLAY A-10

A lot of people play ace-anything, and against those types of players an A-10 is a reasonable hand. But beware—against solid, reasonable players who raise from early position with quality hands only, A-10 is a trouble hand that should be ducked.

If you're in the small blind with A-10, you can attack the big blind with the hand when no one else is in the pot. When you are in the big blind with A-10, you can see the flop against a late position raiser. If the raiser is on the button and is someone who has raised with all sorts of goofy hands, you might consider reraising just to keep him off balance. You don't want him to get in the habit of trying to run over you thinking that you're only going to call his raises.

From late position when you're the first one in the pot, feel free to attack the blinds with A-10. If there is one limper in the pot, particularly if he limps in with a lot of marginal hands, you might consider raising the pot even if you expect him to call the raise. With two limpers already in the pot, it's not a great idea to raise with A-10, whether suited or not.

When the A-10 is suited, it has more value, but in any raised pot, A-10 suited or unsuited must be played with caution. If you are the raiser and get played with, you have to be careful with the hand even when you flop to it. You're hoping to flop a 10 rather than an ace, because you have the boss kicker when you flop a 10. The perfect flop, of course, is K-Q-J because that will hit a lot of people. If someone is playing Q-J, K-Q, or K-J, they have flopped two pair against your made straight, and they probably will have problems getting away from their hands. With two pair, they have four outs, and only three outs—for a tie—if they have a pair and a straight draw.

A trouble flop is when you hit a part of the flop and you're not sure where you stand with your A-10. For example, if the flop comes J-10-2, you've flopped second pair. You may have the best hand on the flop, but with two connecting cards on the board, not only are you beaten by anyone with a jack, but anyone with a hand such as K-Q or 9-8 has a lot of outs to improve to the best hand and beat you on the turn or river. How do you play the hand against this flop?

If you have brought it in for a raise from late position and it's checked to you, you can bet the hand and see what develops. You can always back off if you get too much heat. But as long as your opponents are playing passively, and especially if a non-threatening card comes on the turn (a 4, for example), you can bet the hand again if everyone checks to you. If you get check-raised on the turn, you'll have to give him credit for a jack because people usually won't risk their valuable tournament chips on a check-raise bluff with one to come.

Unless you have some sort of straight possibility to go with your second-pair, you generally should fold when someone makes this type of play. If you're up against an action player who you think is capable of making this play, you may want to call him down. Another alternative is to just check on fourth street and see what he does on the river. If he bets, you call. If he checks, you bet.

You like your hand better if the pot has not been raised before the flop. A lot of times, people automatically check to the raiser, and if one of your opponents has a jack (or another top pair), he probably will check-raise you. But if the pot has not been raised before the flop, he usually will lead at it on the flop, giving you a better indication of where you stand.

Another dangerous situation for your A-10 occurs when you flop an ace, someone bets in front of you, you raise, and a player cold-calls behind you. Suppose the flop comes A-9-7. It is unlikely that someone has a 9-7 or 10-8 (although it's possible), and, of course, it's possible that someone could be playing a suited ace and has made two pair. But generally, you are more concerned about an opponent having an ace with a bigger kicker.

If you are the first to act you can lead at the pot, but if a player raises behind you, you must reevaluate. Do you want to continue with the hand? If the reraiser is a solid player and you can't put him on a draw because you know that he would only call a raise with an A-J or better, you probably should fold.

When you flop an ace to your A-10, it's always more dangerous in a raised pot. When the pot has not been raised, it is less likely that you're against an A-K, A-Q, or A-J and you're more likely to continue with the hand. How you proceed always depends on the pre-flop action: Even though there are no exposed cards like there are in seven-card stud, there is a lot of information that you can gather in hold'em.

The information that you gather from the pre-flop action determines how strongly you can play A-10 and how long you stay in when you flop an ace. For example, when you are playing against only one opponent in an unraised pot, he could easily have a weaker kicker than your 10. He may think that because the pot was not raised pre-flop, you also have a weak kicker and his has you beat. So, you don't have to automatically abandon the hand if he bets—just hope that he didn't hit his weak kicker on the flop. If he's the type of player who makes a habit of playing ace-anything, you might want to just check-call, gritting your teeth along the way in the hope that he hasn't hit his kicker.

32. HOW TO PLAY K-9

K-9 suited is a typical "temptation" hand. It looks fairly good but it can lead you into a world of trouble. In wide-open hold'em tournaments some people will play king-anything suited, and the 9 gives the hand some straight potential, even though it's a three-gap hand. Of course, when you flop a straight to it, like Q-J-10—you can be beaten by anyone holding A-K.

You must be selective about how you play this hand—it's not one that you can take heat with. Against an early-position raiser, K-9 suited is not a playable hand. From early to middle position, whether or not the pot has been raised, this hand is a chip burner.

If you're in the big blind and someone has raised the pot with several callers, you can defend your blind for the single raise. From the small blind, pass in a raised pot, but you might call for one half-bet in an unraised pot and see what develops on the flop. Heads-up against the big blind you can raise with K-9, as it figures to be a better hand. When you are in late position and several people have limped in, you can do the same.

If you are getting close to the money table, K-9 is not the type of hand that you want to take a risk with if you are low on chips. If you're in a desperate situation—for example, the blinds will eat you up in a few hands—you may want to take a stand with K-9 from late position. Not because you like the hand, but because playing K-9 appears to be a better option than playing the fast approaching blinds all-in.

What if you flop either a flush or a flush draw to K-9 suited? If you flop a flush you should play this hand very aggressively. You arc holding thc sccond nuts and generally will win with it. Of course, if the ace and two other cards of your suit come, you have the nuts and can play it accordingly. You can check-call on the flop and then raise on fourth or fifth street, or you can lead and hope to get raised. Play it any way that you think will get the most bets from the table.

If you flop a flush draw, your position should dictate how you play from there. In an unraised pot from early position, check-call if the pot is multiway, and check-raise if you're heads-up. In late position with a decent stack of chips, you usually can raise to create a bigger pot. Your raise usually will get you a free card on the turn because your opponents will often check to the raiser on fourth street no matter what card comes. You have to consider the possibility that someone is drawing to the nut flush, and the play at your table usually will dictate where you stand.

33. HOW TO PLAY 10-6

Another three-gap hand that some players like to play when it is suited is a hand such as 10-6 (and even J-7 or 9-5). Although the 10 has some straight potential, this hand falls into the category of two-gap unsuited hands, in that even if you flop a straight to it, someone could have a better straight. For example, suppose the flop comes 9-8-7. Since people habitually play J-10, you could be in a world of hurt with your second-best straight.

When you are tempted to play these types of hands, ask yourself "What am I hoping to make?" At least with a hand like K-9 suited you can make a high flush, but the best that you can do with 10-6 suited is make a low flush that is vulnerable to higher flushes and a second-best straight. Unless you catch a flop like 10-10-6, you're asking for trouble when you play hands like this.

About the only time that it's playable is for one half-bet in the small blind or the mandatory single bet in the big blind (in unraised pots). If someone raises before you must act from the big blind, the only reason you might call is when five or six people already are in the pot. Even then, it is a questionable call because you must flop perfectly to it. Certainly you don't lose much by passing.

Flopping top pair to 10-6 can be dangerous business. Suppose you're in the big blind in an unraised pot and you flop top pair. Against only one or two opponents you might lead at the hand to see whether it's good. But with more than two other people in the pot you check. A lot of people like to play hands that have a 10 in them, so if one of your three or four opponents has a 10, his kicker most likely is higher than your lowly 6.

Sometimes you will see people defending their blind with hands like 10-6 suited against a late-position raiser. But even if the raiser has a weak hand, yours probably isn't any better—and he has position on you after the flop. Why force yourself, after catching a little piece of the flop, to have to make a lot of tricky decisions? Part of the value of this book is to help you avoid these type of situations

PLAYING THE BLINDS

34. BIG AND LITTLE BLINDS

The most expensive hand that you ever will play in a limit hold'em tournament is the hand that you get for free in the big blind, or the one that costs you only half a bet more in the small blind. More tournament players have crippled themselves by defending a blind that they should not have played, or by playing in the blind more aggressively than they should when they flop something marginal, than for any other reason.

What often happens is that you catch part of the flop and become involved with a hand that you wouldn't have played had you not been in the blind. With a holding such as Q♠ 8♠, your thinking may go something like this: "This isn't that great a hand, but there

are several people in the pot and it's only going to cost me half a bet to call." A fast or
unknowledgeable player then makes the mistake of betting the hand aggressively when he
flops a queen, when a better option is to just
check and see what kind of action takes place
behind him. If someone raises his bet, he then
is faced with a quandary: "Should I call the
raise or pass?"

Playing the blinds correctly requires ex-
treme prudence and discretion. The number
of opponents in the pot, the playing styles of
your opponents, and the nature of the flop are
key factors. If one of your adversaries is the
type who would raise to try to get a free card
if the flop offers him a straight or flush draw,
you might continue playing when you flop top
pair with your Q♠ 8♠. But if there is no logi-
cal draw on the flop other than top pair/top
kicker or trips, and if you have no other reasonable outs, you must give serious consideration to just passing his raise.

Troublesome blind hands are even trickier
to play when you catch part of the flop in a
raised pot. With a hand such as A♥ 8♥ for
example, you must proceed cautiously if you
flop an ace. Against any substantial action,
you are better off to just give up. The stron-
gest hand that you can hope to flop (aside
from a made flush) is top pair with a flush

draw. Be willing to go for the river if the flop comes A♦ K♥ 4♥ for example. However, if you are subjected to any type of substantial action, you may be forced to just check-call rather than lead; although, as long as you are not raised, you can continue to take the lead. If your flush fails to materialize on the river, you can just check and then decide whether to pay off an opponent who bets.

Against a single opponent who has only called all the way, you may as well bet if you intend to call anyway, unless you believe that he might raise you. If you indeed think that he may raise, it would be wise to check him, thus avoiding being bluffed out of the pot, and also giving yourself an opportunity to snap up the pot if your hand is better than his. Checking on the river sometimes can induce a bluff. Your apparent weakness may tempt your opponent to bet when he actually has been on a draw and holds only a lower pair than you do.

Playing blind against blind is more likely to happen from the middle rounds of a tournament onward than in the opening stages. Any two cards 10 and higher are worth a raise from the small blind against the big blind, or if you are the big blind and the small blind has only called. Ace-x is worth a raise in a small blind-big blind confrontation, or against a small blind that has limped into the pot. It usually is correct to raise with these hands, regardless of chip count.

An important concept in blind-against-blind action is the "bunching factor." If a lot of people have passed, it is likely that none of them are holding big cards. It then becomes more likely that one of the blind hands does have big cards, so be aware that one of the blinds may wake up with a premium hand in these situations.

Some people cannot be bluffed, although this is a less frequent occurrence in tournaments than it is in ring games. If you think that a player will defend his blind very liberally (he is what I call a "bluff-proof" blind protector), you should base your betting strategy strictly on the merits of your hand, rather than on trying to run over someone who won't lay down a hand no matter what. Trying to bluff a player who is bluff-proof can be a costly tournament error.

Be very hesitant about raising from the small or big blind with multiple players in the pot. Against five or more players, your raise must be based strictly on the merits of your hand. Occasionally, you will see players raising with small to medium pairs. Although the raise is a way to build a big pot, you will be forced to flop a set to have your hand stand up in multiway action. Therefore, it makes little sense to raise with these hands unless you're in a gambling mood.

One time that you might raise from the big blind with small to medium pairs is when you are almost all in and several people already are in the pot. With a "What the hell!" attitude, you can fire in your last chips on a raise, knowing that no matter what comes, you will be getting multiway action on your money, with odds of hitting your set at 7.5 to 1 on the flop and 4 to 1 if you go to the river. With an average stack, you are better off just calling from the big blind, hoping to hit your set. If you are in the small blind with only a few chips remaining, you probably should wait for the button.

Starting hand requirements with which you can defend the small blind can be more liberal in unraised pots than in raised pots. In raised pots you can call from the small blind with small pairs and suited connectors when five or more people are in the pot, including yourself and the big blind. It will cost only your original half-bet plus one extra bet. Suited cards with two gaps and straight potential such as 8♠ 5♠, 9♥ 6♥ or 10♣ 7♣ are another type of hand that you can play for an additional half-bet, but only when there are several people in the pot.

PLAYING AGAINST SUPER-AGGRESSORS

by Tom McEvoy

35. STRATEGY ADJUSTMENTS

In *Championship Hold'em*, T.J. Cloutier and I defined some of the changes in the way that tournaments and cash games are being played today. One of those changes has been brought about by the playing style of the Super Aggressors, bandits who can steal your chips even when they don't have a lock hand. They are the ones who constantly put a lot of pressure on their opponents, and they pick up a lot of pots that are "up for sale" when their more conservative opponents show weakness.

Super Aggressors are always firing away at these "ownerless" pots and they're winning a fair number of them, because, although their opponents know that they're probably stealing, they don't have enough of a hand themselves to put up a fight.

Super Aggressors play much more aggressively before the flop with a lot of hands—and they aren't always premium. They play position very strongly and don't need as much of a hand to bring it in for a raise, especially when they're the first one in the pot. They either raise or fold, and they three-bet a lot of marginal hands. If a Super Aggressor thinks that someone is out of line with a late position raise, he will come over the top of the raiser, even with hands such as Q-10 or a pair of deuces.

Super Aggressors are also willing to check-raise with nothing, which is very hard to pull off, and requires immense skill. Although this kamikaze style often will cause the Super Aggressor to crash and burn early in the tournament, it also can help him amass a lot of chips if some of his hands hold up.

In multiway pots, the Super Aggressor will gamble with all sorts of strange hands before the flop. For example, he might call two or three bets cold with an 8-6 suited or a small pair—he's willing to gamble in the hope of catching a favorable flop. Super-aggressive players will play any pair, sometimes bringing it in for a raise, and I've seen them cap the pot with hands like 10-10 or K-8 suited.

When the flop comes raggedy, Super Aggressors bet A-K even though all they have is overcards, a strategy that I think is generally a mistake. Suppose there are about five people in the pot and the flop comes 9-4-2 with three different suits. Continuing to be aggressive with A-K in this scenario is a mistake because someone is going to have something. I don't agree with that kind of play, but we have to deal with it in today's faster, more aggressive tournament action.

These Super Aggressors are almost always younger than 40, fearless, and aggressive to the point that they either fold or raise with marginal hands (rather than just calling with them). In other words, they aren't playing "by the book." That is, they aren't gauging their play by "Group I" hands, "Group II" hands, position, and so on.

Most of these players play their poker in California. Although Asian players have been typecast as Super Aggressors, there really isn't any correlation to race. Super Aggressors are most likely to intimidate players that are older, more conservative, and less experienced, as well as women. (Note, however, that although women in general are more conservative, some are every bit as aggressive as men.)

The style of the Super Aggressor tends to throw more cautious players off their game by moving them out of their comfort zone. The Cautious Conservative is not comfortable playing in games where people are reraising with pocket fours and 10-8. The aggressive players who fit the kamikaze profile are unpredictable to their more traditional opponents, whose ability to read other players decrease because they can't put their aggressive opponents on specific hands, and wind up giving action when they're beaten.

At the same time, the Cautious Conservatives are *more* predictable with their "A-B-C" style of traditional tournament play. The Super Aggressor, who looks like a wild man to the Cautious Conservative, is able to read his traditional opponents much better than they are reading him, which, of course, is a huge advantage. In fact some Super Aggressors don't have a lot of respect for the older champions and think they can run over their more seasoned opponents.

So, how can we traditionalists adjust our play to contend with and defend against the Super Aggressors? One thing you can do is to call people down with less strength than you ordinarily would, especially when you're putting them on a hand like A-K and think that they're betting with overcards only. Another play you can make is to check-raise with second pair, particularly when the game is shorthanded. For example, suppose you have two tens and one overcard comes on the flop. If a very aggressive player keeps firing at you, you might simply call him down. In the past I wasn't keen on engaging them, but these days I do, and, quite often, I have the best hand.

Since I am known as a more traditional tournament player, I decided it was time to refine my style to better compete in today's more aggressive tournaments. I'm willing to make some adjustments in my play and change my game around if it means getting better tournament results. Specifically, I have experimented by playing online hold'em in $15-$30 shorthanded games.

I've been playing a much more aggressive style than I am accustomed to, and although I've had some big swings, for the most part I have made a lot of money by opening up my game and playing a very fast style. I look for shorthanded games, something I never used to do. I will deliberately try to find a three or four-handed game, and I'll even start a game heads-up. I've also been trying to profile other online players in an effort to get a line on everybody's play, especially the weaker players. For example, I look for certain players that I know are fast and loose and try to get position on them, avoiding the players that I know are tough and have been very successful in shorthanded games.

Are these super-aggressive tournament aces for real? They are, but not everyone can play like they do and get the same results. That's because they're not only aggressive, but also very skillful tournament pros.

Here's the bottom line: If you can't beat 'em, try joining 'em. There's a reason why some of the new breed of tournament players with their super-aggressive style are successful. Yes, they crash and burn more often than not, but when they get there, they get there with chips—and they know how to win. They may have only a few firsts and a lot of last-place finishes, but those firsts are worth a whole lot.

Can today's Super Aggressors sustain their good results over the long haul? The answer is not clear-cut—they've had a lot of success the last few years, but it's hard to tell where they'll be ten years from now.

NO-LIMIT
HOLD'EM
HANDS

I

INTRODUCTION

No-limit hold'em is today's biggest tournament game. We have television, the Internet, satellites, and Chris Moneymaker to thank for the explosion in popularity of poker's most thrilling game. In what other game can an amateur parlay a $39 satellite win into a $2.5 million payday, as Moneymaker did in his 2003 championship run?

"If he can do it, I can do it!" is the idea that has encouraged millions of novice poker players to take a shot at international fame and instant wealth by playing no-limit hold'em tournaments.

And why not?

All it takes is skill, practice, good judgment, a lot of heart, and a little bit of luck.

Because so many new players are entering

no-limit hold'em tournaments in this new age of poker, you will be facing a wider range of tournament skill levels than ever before. You can't depend on your opponents to play by the book and make standard moves at the pot. Making the right decision in every hand you play is more important than ever because every time you enter a pot in no-limit hold'em, you are putting your entire stack of chips at risk.

You don't have to win a lot of pots in no-limit hold'em; you just need to win most of the pots you play. And to win those pots, you cannot afford to make mistakes. In no-limit hold'em, where all your chips can be lost in one hand, only one or two errors in judgment are enough to doom your chances of winning or even finishing in the money.

We have designed the sample hands in this section to allow you to practice the decision-making skills you'll need to win at no-limit hold'em. We hope that by studying these practice hands, you will better understand the mental processes that professional no-limit hold'em players use to determine the best way to play certain types of hands in various situations against different types of opponents.

Look at each hand and think about how you would play it given the various scenarios that can occur. Then read the analysis that T.J. gives for the play of the hand and compare it with your ideas.

In each example, Player A is the first to act, Player B is the next, and Player C is last.

ACES

36. HOW TO PLAY ACES
IN FRONT POSITION

There's an old saying in poker that aces win small pots and lose big pots. In this section you'll see that this old adage is a fallacy—*when* you play aces the right way in *all* situations. Let's start with how to play A-A from a front position.

There are two schools of thought on how to play aces from a front position. A lot of players like to limp with two aces in the hope that someone will raise and give them the chance to play back at them so they can win a raised pot. They might win it right there, or they might get played with and wind up winning a huge pot. I don't like to give any free cards, so I prefer playing aces the second way — raising with them right away.

THE CASE FOR LIMPING

For years I have maintained that if you limp with two aces, and you don't get raised, you should not lose any more money than what you've already put in. If someone comes swinging at the pot after the flop, you can release the hand. What have you lost? Nothing except the original bet that you limped in with. But I've seen a lot of players limp in with aces, get a flop such as 7-6-5 — and then somebody who got in there cheap with something like 6-5 or 9-8 swings at the pot, and the limper pays him off. This is not a good idea. Don't let him in to begin with. If you're going to limp, play it strong if you think you have the best hand. Otherwise, let it go.

Suppose you limp in with aces and get three or four callers. If the flop comes 4-4-2 (or includes any other pair), be leery. Any time a pair comes when you've limped, or three connecting cards flop, or three suited cards flop that don't match one of your aces, be very careful how you play. These scenarios can easily trip you up when you limp with aces.

Be aware that when you limp in and no one raises, there will always be random blind hands that can show you any two cards and you never know when someone has hit something. If you bring it in for a raise, though, you can be more specific about putting people on certain hands, or at least taking them off of them.

THE CASE FOR RAISING

You want to limit the field when you play big pairs so that, ideally, you can play against only one or two opponents. When you raise before the flop, you usually will have only one opponent. You know that you have the best hand to start with, and even though you might get unlucky and see the other guy make a set, that's just part of poker. Bad things can happen to good hands.

If someone calls your raise with A-K, A-Q, or A-J they are in a heap of trouble, and right where you want them. This is why I prefer raising with pocket aces. If someone plays back at you, you have the chance to win a big pot. You raise and he reraises—now you have to decide whether you want to come over the top, or slow-play your aces. In other words, do you want to shut him out right there or do you want to play the pot with him? A lot of times, I'll play him a pot. But if I get reraised and a third player calls the reraise, I'll move in — I don't necessarily want to play two opponents, I want to win the pot right there or at least get heads up.

When you make raises, don't tip the strength of your hand by the size of your bet. Raise the same amount every time. Obviously the amount of the raise will differ at each level of the tournament, because as you get deeper the blinds are higher and there's more money involved. If you're going to raise $400 with A-K, for example, raise $400 on two aces.

There are a lot of players on the circuit who vary their bets depending on the value of their cards — which means that you can tell what they have by how much they wager. Often, they'll make a smaller raise with aces than they ordinarily would because they want to get played with. There also are a lot of limit hold'em players who are new to no-limit hold'em who move all in with two aces, trying to win the antes. Neither play makes sense — the whole idea of poker is to get as much value as you can get from your hand, and neither play helps you do that.

Now let's look at three scenarios that

demonstrate how you might play pocket aces from early position when you are the first player in the pot.

SCENARIO ONE

You are Player A, sitting in early position and have been dealt:

You limp into the pot. The player next to the button raises. The button and both of the blinds fold. You decide to just call. The flop comes:

Now what do you do? Since you have set things up to slow-play your hand, you check. Player B bets. You flat call.

The turn card is the 2♠:

You check. Player B puts in a big bet, and you raise, knowing that there's a good chance that you'll get played with if Player B has something like A-K or a pocket pair such as queens or jacks. Player B calls. The river comes with another deuce:

You bet. Player B calls and shows A♠ K♠. He had top pair with the nut flush draw on the turn. Because you limped, he probably thought that he had the best hand by a long shot, or at the very least a tie. He didn't put you on a set, and it wouldn't even occur to most players that you might have two aces. This is the perfect scenario for slow-playing pocket aces and getting full value, and it's one way to trap your opponent. Now let's look at a different style of slow-playing aces from early position.

SCENARIO TWO

You are Player A. This time you raise from early position with your pocket aces. Player B reraises, and you flat call. The board comes the same as Scenario One.

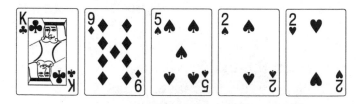

When the flop comes K-9-5, you are thinking, "How can I get the most out of this pot?" If you lead at the pot, Player B probably will raise if he has A-K You don't want him to fold, so you don't make a huge bet, putting in the amount that you believe he will call if he has any kind of hand. Whether he calls or raises, you have him trapped (unless, of course, he has pocket kings, in which case you're the one who is trapped). You lead at this hand all the way through—his pre-flop reraise and call on the flop tell you that he is pot-committed. In this situation, your pre-flop raise built a decent pot for you to win.

SCENARIO THREE

You are Player A. You raise from early position with A-A, Player B reraises, and Player C cold calls the reraise. Now what do you do?

In this situation, you know that Player C has a big hand, probably K-K or Q-Q, so you go over the top with an all-in bet. There's plenty of money in the pot already, so you simply move on it. You hope for a call, but even if Player B or C don't you still have won a decent pot.

Now suppose that you reraise Player C's raise, Player B folds, and Player C calls your reraise. The flop comes the same as in Scenarios One and Two. At this point you have two options: You either lead at it all the way, or you just move in on the flop. You want to get paid off on your aces, but even if Player C does not call, you've still won a big pot with your aggressive play of pocket aces from up front.

PLAYING ACES IN THE LATE STAGE

Suppose you're playing in the late stages of a tournament and somebody has raised in front of you. Now you must make the decision as to whether you want to move all in or just make a reraise that you think he will call, and get his money later. Say that you reraised and the board comes 9 high. If he has two jacks, is he the type of player who will lead at it? Think about all of this before you make your reraise.

A good player always trys to extract as much money as he can from a hand. If he's a really good player, you might as well just move him in and see if he wants to play the hand; if he's just average, you might want to just reraise an amount that you think he will call. If you've put him on a decent pocket pair, you hope for a small flop so that you can pick up the rest of his chips. Again, you play each type of player differently.

POT-LIMIT HOLD'EM

In pot-limit hold'em, you can't put as much pressure on the pot as in no-limit, but you still want to raise with aces to start building a pot and protect your hand a little better after the flop. The idea of pot-limit is to get enough chips in there to protect your hand later. You can be called by a lot of strange hands, so good players are always in there trying to take off big pairs or big hands.

I play aces the same way in both games. I might limp once in a while just to change my play in no-limit, but I would never limp with aces in pot-limit for one reason: I always want to build a pot. You don't want to be in a pot where there is hardly anything in on the flop, because then you can't bet enough to get anyone out—you want to be in a situation where you can control the hand, and can dictate the action. Your pre-flop raise will help put you in control on the flop.

37. HOW TO PLAY ACES IN MIDDLE POSITION

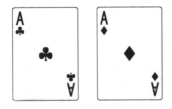

If the pot is opened or raised in the first three seats, you have two options: You can reraise, or you can play "second-hand low." Suppose you're in a real action game, and four or five players—including you—limp in, before a guy who raises every pot puts in a raise. In other words, there might be four or five limpers before anybody raises the pot, and you have set him up to play second-hand low. The first player in the pot might have a decent hand, but you have aces. The first player or the original raiser might reraise the pot and now you have a big pot to win before the flop. So if you reraise right there, they might figure that you are just trying to pick up the pot, or you have A-K, or something like that. They hardly ever put you on aces when you play second-hand low.

You know that you have a real action player behind you, so when somebody leads into the pot in front of you, you just call. You suspect that the original limper might also have a big hand, so you're setting the stage to raise both the limper and the action player. You're trying to trap everybody, and you want to make them pay to try to draw out on your aces.

Even if the first player in the pot brings it in for a raise, you still play second-hand low by just flat-calling his raise in the hope that someone behind you (most likely the action player) will reraise. If that doesn't happen, there's still a chance that the player who raised up front will come after you on the flop.

In fact, if you have several action players in the game, you can even play third-hand low if all of the action players are sitting behind you. You can be the third limper. You can pull it off even if it's raised and called in front of you, in which case you can also flat-call with the intention of reraising if one of the action players raises behind you. Naturally, you have to really know your opponents to pull off this play.

SCENARIO ONE

You are in middle position with A♠ A♣. You raised the pot before the flop, and were called by Player B on the button and Player C in the big blind. The flop comes:

You make a standard bet in the hope of getting called by A-Q, K-Q, Q-J, Q-10, a 9 with a big kicker, or J-10 (straight draw), or someone with a diamond draw. You could get beaten by these drawing hands or by the pair hands if they double-pair with their kicker. But in all of these scenarios, you're still the favorite on the flop. The only drawing hand better off than your aces would be J♦ 10♦, and even that's only slightly favored.

The fourth street card is the 5♥.

Make sure that you bet enough on the turn to put pressure on your opponents. You want to force them to decide whether they want to commit a lot of money to this pot. Obviously you are a good favorite over all the hands mentioned. The 2♥ comes at the river.

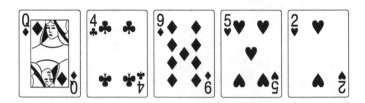

At the river, if anyone has stayed in the hand, I would empty out (bet all my chips) hoping to get called. The way that the hand has been played should indicate that A-A is still the best hand. In this scenario, I did not forget about the possibility that somebody flopped a set, but because of the straight and flush possibilities on board, I am sure that if anyone had flopped a set, he would have moved on the flop, or certainly on fourth street.

SCENARIO TWO— PLAYING SECOND-HAND LOW

Before the flop, one player limps in from an early position. You know from his previous play that he could be holding anything. You are the next to act, with A♣ A♦. You decide to just call, while the button, the small blind, and the big blind also flat-call.

The flop comes:

The two blinds and the early limper check, and you do the same. The button bets, the two blinds fold, and the original limper calls. Obviously you don't know exactly what the button and the limper have, but you do know that you have the best possible hand. Therefore, you have two choices: Do you flat-call, knowing that you have disguised the strength of your hand, in the hope of winning a huge pot on fourth or fifth street? Or do you raise the pot on the flop so as not to give any free cards? Let's take a look at two possible scenarios.

CHOICE A—
FLAT CALL ON THE FLOP

Along with the early-position limper, you flat-called the button's bet on the flop.

The turn card is the 10♣.

Now you have them where you want them, and it's time to get the most value from your hand. If the limper checks, lead at the pot with a decent bet, hoping to either get raised or called by one, if not both of your opponents. Now if either player raises, he has committed himself to the pot. In that case, you go on the offensive and move all in. You know that there is a very good chance that at least one of them is on a big draw, has flopped a set, or has top two pair. If one of them calls your all-in bet and the river comes:

How sweet it is!

But what if either or both opponents flat call on the turn? In that case, on fifth street when you know that you have the nuts, you bet the amount that you think they will call. You don't move in because you don't want them to throw their hands away, you simply want to get full value from your aces. The difference between good and average players is that a good player always does whatever it takes to get full value from a hand.

CHOICE B—RAISE ON THE FLOP

Now suppose that you choose to raise the pot right on the flop so as not to give any free cards, but still with the hope that either or both opponent call. Understand that if either opponent calls the raise, his hand would have to be a set, top two pair, top and bottom pair, A-K or A-Q, a flush draw, or a pair with a flush draw. (In this case, if someone has a pair and a flush draw, he would have to have an ace and a flush draw.) Let's say that both the limper and the button call your raise. Again, the board looks like this on fourth street:

The limper checks, so you make a big bet, looking to either win the pot right there or get called by one or both opponents. Suppose the button calls and the limper folds. Again the 5♠ comes at the river. This time you are the first to act—what do you do? It's time for the kill! You've put him on a big hand and now you want to find out just how important it is to him, so you shove in all your chips. Does life get much sweeter than this?

After the hand is over, you discover that the limper had the K♥ Q♥ and the button had the A♥ 5♥. The button probably stayed to the river because he put you on a flush draw and when he paired his kicker, he hoped that his two pair (aces and fives) would win a big pot for him.

SETTING THE STANDARD RAISE

Every time the limit increases in no-limit tournaments the first person that puts in a raise generally sets the standard for the amount that everybody else is going to raise during that level. For example, if the first raise is $300, that becomes the standard raise that everyone makes. But when I play, I try to break the standard. If the going rate is $300, I might make my standard raise $400. I want to be called, so every time I raise I put in my standard amount, not theirs. Again, I don't want to tip the value of my hand.

38. HOW TO PLAY ACES IN LATE POSITION

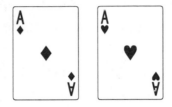

You always raise with aces from a late position. After everyone has passed to the button, you sometimes will see people limp with pocket aces, but I think that's a horrible play. The chances of someone raising from the two blinds are slim, since you have two of the four aces in the deck locked up. And if they don't raise they're going to get free cards on the flop with any kind of hand, and you will have no idea of where you are with your aces. All considered, I think that you definitely should raise with aces when you're in late position.

It doesn't matter how many people are in the pot—you should raise, period. If someone has raised in front of you with a lot of players in the pot, you're going to reraise. You cannot give free cards very often in a tournament if you want to survive. A lot of times your opponents will discount the strength of a late-position raise and will play with you because they believe you're on a steal.

Make your standard raise if you're the first one in the pot, or if there's only one limper in front of you, but if more than one player is already in you should consider pushing all your chips to the center of the table. Any time that you have pocket aces you want someone to come after you, coming over the top. Then your decision is whether to just flat-call and try to nail him after the flop, or move in immediately to try to win the pot right there. If you flat-call, there's always the danger that your opponent will out-flop you, but when you're playing aces in no-limit poker, you should always choose the bolder strategy, to try to get as much out of the hand as possible.

39. HOW TO PLAY ACES IN THE BLINDS

When you have aces in one of the blinds, it is more important to raise than it is in any other position, because you always have to act first after the flop. You're in the weakest position at the start of the hand, so you need to play aces right, which means raising.

Suppose everybody checks to the button. He raises and the small blind folds. You're sitting in the big blind with aces. In this situation you might try to trap him by just flat-calling the raise in the hope that something will come on the flop that hits him a little bit but hits you even better. The best scenario that you're hoping for is that your opponent has something like A-6.

Pocket aces is such a powerful hand that you raise with them most of the time from any position, period. Here's a good example of what sometimes happens when you limp with aces. In the last hand of the World Series of Poker in 2001, Dewey Tomko and Carlos Mortensen were heads-up at the final table. Dewey limped with two aces on the button (the small blind), and Carlos raised $70,000 with the K♣ Q♣. Dewey decided to just flat-call.

The flop came J♦ 10♣ 3♣. If Dewey had not had two aces, Carlos would have been a slight favorite on the flop. But since Dewey had two of the aces that Carlos needed to make a straight, Carlos was only a slight dog with two cards to come. He had 26 wins (13 outs twice)—a nine, an ace, any club, or runner-runner to beat two aces. Against any other hand except pocket aces Carlos would have had 30 outs. He would have even had 30 outs against a set, but not against aces since they were two of his win cards. If Dewey had had two jacks in the hole, Carlos would have had more outs than he did against the aces.

Carlos bet $100,000 on the flop and Dewey raised $400,000. Carlos reraised without hesitation, moving in all his chips. Dewey called, so all the money was in the middle on the flop. It came down to two aces against a double draw for a flush or straight. The drawing hand won when a 9 came at the river and Carlos became the World Champion of Poker.

Nothing was wrong with Dewey's slow-play of the aces—he got the action he wanted from Carlos. But Carlos got the type of flop he needed and Dewey's pocket rockets went down in flames.

WHEN BAD THINGS HAPPEN TO GOOD HANDS

At the Legends of Poker tournament at the Bicycle Club John Hom raised the pot, and the button moved all in. I was in the little blind with two red aces and called all-in. Hom had more money than me, and knowing that I wouldn't go all-in without a huge hand, Hom laid down his two black kings. The button had A-K offsuit. Now I had a huge percentage of the deck in my favor. The board finished with four spades and the button won it with the A♠ and knocked me out of the tournament. Hom had thrown away the K♠, so even he could have beaten my aces with a king-high flush.

At the no-limit championship event at the Bike, Phil Hellmuth had just bluffed at me and I had doubled up with two pair. I looked down and saw that I had two aces, so I brought it in for the standard raise. Phil was in the big blind and I knew that he was hot as hell because he doubled me up. Sure enough, when it gets to him he says, "All in!" and bets $6,400 more. I called. He had A-Q offsuit against my two aces. The board came K-10-4-J-x, and I was out of that tournament. Amazing! But that's aces for you.

ACE-KING

40. HOW TO PLAY ACE-KING

To win a no-limit hold'em tournament, you have to win with A-K and you have to beat A-K. Although it may not come on the final hand, A-K often will be the *deciding* hand, the one with which you win or lose the most chips. Big Slick is the biggest "decision" hand in tournament play.

In this section, which we adapted from our book *Championship No-Limit & Pot-Limit Hold'em*, we will discuss various tournament scenarios and how to play A-K according to the situation.

At a no-limit tournament table, Player A raised $1,200 before the flop. You are Player B and reraise $1,200 with an A-K offsuit. Sitting behind you, Player C cold-calls your reraise, and Player A also calls.

The flop comes:

SCENARIO ONE

Player A bets $8,000 on the flop.

What is your best move?

If I was Player B, I would have flat-called the $1,200 to see what comes on the flop, or, if I had enough chips, raised about four times that amount. You, then, would put in a big enough raise to shut out the rest of the field so that you can play head up against one opponent. If you make a large raise, the original raiser could throw his hand away and you will win the pot right there, or maybe he'd call. In either case, your raise probably will freeze out the rest of the field.

But Player B didn't do that. He let Player C into the pot (who even cold-called B's raise), so Player B has to give both Players A and

Player C credit for having good hands.

Player A bets $8,000 on the flop. I would fold at this point; first of all, Player A has either A-A, A-K, Q-Q, A-Q, or, if he's a loose player, two sevens. Since I have the K, I don't put him on a spade draw. Secondly, since Player C cold called behind me, he also could have flopped a set. As a result, I would fold the A-K.

SCENARIO TWO

Player A checks on the flop, so you do as well.

SCENARIO THREE

Player A moves all-in on the flop.
What's your best move?
Pass.

ANALYSIS

Some of the key elements for analysis are missing from this scenario—for example, how many players are at the table; whether this hand comes up in the early, middle, or late stage of the tournament; and what you know about your opponents. You should know which players will raise or reraise with A-J or A-Q, and who won't raise unless they have aces or king—because you have been studying them while you were playing. If your opponent is the type that won't raise with a weak hand, you don't have anything with the A-K, so why not get rid of it?

Now suppose that you have $2,500 in front of you, and you bring it in for $1,500. Then somebody reraises behind you. You are pot-committed and you go on with the hand, because you have more than one-half of your chips already in the pot. An experienced player often will pot-commit by putting in most of his chips when he raises because he knows that if he gets reraised, he will automatically go for the rest of it. A less experienced player might think that he can blow the raiser off the hand by reraising—that the raiser will save that extra $500 or $1,000 that he has left. What the inexperienced reraiser doesn't realize is that the only reason that the raiser has pot-committed is so that he can't get away from the hand.

41. HOW TO PLAY ACE-KING

Let's fill in the missing elements. You are playing in a $1,000 buy-in tournament. It's the middle stage of the tournament and you're at a full table. Player A raises $1,200 before the flop. You are Player B, sitting in fifth position with four players behind you. You reraise $4,800. Player C cold calls the reraise for $6,000, and Player A calls.

The flop comes:

SCENARIO ONE

Player A checks on the flop, putting you in a quandary. You have top pair and the nut flush draw, and there is $18,000 in the pot. This could be the perfect trap hand, but you have to play it, so you move in with all of your chips. You can't beat a set, of course, but you're still drawing to the nut flush. It doesn't matter what Player C does—you're going to play the hand anyway.

SCENARIO TWO

Player A bets. What do you do?

Again, you move all-in. You can't hope for a better flop, unless it had come A-A-K. This is a flop that you have to play.

42. HOW TO PLAY ACE-KING

Once again, you have been dealt Big Slick. The tournament conditions and pre-flop action are the same as they were in the previous example.

Your hand is:

The flop comes:

SCENARIO ONE

Player A bets and from watching him carefully you know that he's pretty good. So, you pass with your A-K.

Why? Because a lot of times good players will make a move with a big hand, trying to induce you into playing back at them. Since it's clear that Player A knows what he's doing, you should throw the hand away.

SCENARIO TWO

Player A checks. What is your best move? If Player A checks, you check too. Then if Player C bets, you throw the hand away.

ANALYSIS

Tossing your hand is tough to do because you have a lot of money in the pot. But why give up the tournament for one hand? The A-K is a perfect trap hand, unless you're playing at a shorthanded table, which makes it more powerful. If you're playing against five or fewer players, A-K is quite strong, but if you're in a full ring, there are a lot of scenarios when Big Slick amounts to nothing. You want to avoid any traps that you can get into with it.

Two queens is a decent raising hand, one that a lot of players will stand a reraise with (but I'm not one of them). Given this flop, there is a good chance that either Player A or C has flopped quad queens or a full house if either one is holding an A-Q. People think that Big Slick is a big-big hand, but it isn't—in fact, two deuces is a better hand heads-up than A-K: In a computer run of 100,000 hands, two deuces will win more often than A-K in heads-up situations played to a showdown.

43. HOW TO PLAY ACE-KING

You have Big Slick and the flop comes with three baby cards:

SCENARIO ONE

Player A bets, and you throw your hand away, because you have nothing. In no-limit hold'em, you never chase.

SCENARIO TWO

Player A checks. What's your move?
You also check.

SCENARIO THREE

Player A checks, you check, and player C bets. Now what?

You fold, no matter what Player A does after Player C's bet. Again, you never chase with A-K in no-limit hold'em.

Remember that Player C has cold called a reraise before the flop and is still to act after you. It's fairly certain that he can beat a pair of deuces, fours, or sevens, and your A-K can't beat any of those pairs. So, that's another reason why you dump your A-K if he bets.

KINGS

44. HOW TO PLAY KINGS IN EARLY POSITION

Two kings is the second-best pair you can be dealt, but also the most dangerous, because it's a very hard hand to get away from before the flop. Usually, if there is one raise you're going to reraise with two kings. Of course, there is the chance that you will run into two aces, or a big ace, or even "any ace." If somebody with an ace in his hand calls you,

you're a goner if an ace comes on the flop.

Any time the flop is raised and reraised before it gets to you in a tournament, I suggest that you dump your two kings. Even if it takes you out of a winnable pot once in a while, you will save a lot of money in the long run.

Now let's look at a couple of situations when you have been dealt K-K. Suppose you are playing in a $1,000 no-limit tournament and you are in the middle stage of the event. You are Player A, the first to act, and you have been dealt pocket kings. How do you play the hand before the flop?

SCENARIO ONE

You might limp with the two kings from front position, hoping that someone will raise. If somebody behind you has pocket aces, more power to him: If you run into aces, there's nothing you can do about it. The strategy behind limping with kings is to let somebody raise you so that you can reraise and win the pot immediately. If a player just calls, you still have the second-best hand that you can start with, and you're just hoping that an ace doesn't come on the board. The reason why two kings are so hard to play is because it seems that an ace so often comes on the flop when you have the kings.

SCENARIO TWO

Say that you limp with the kings, Player B raises, Player C calls, and you reraise. More likely than not, you will win the pot right there, unless either Player B or C has aces or queens. If either one of them reraises you, you're probably a gone goose. If Player B has aces, for example, he will move you all-in, but if he doesn't there's a pretty good chance that you have the best hand. If Player C reraises, he would have to be a very good player to be check-raising in this situation with pocket aces. It takes a very good player to pull off this play, and you don't see it very often in tournaments. Therefore, it is unlikely that Player C is using this strategy.

45. HOW TO PLAY KINGS ON A RAG FLOP

Let's take a look at a hand that came up during the first level of play at a $10,000 World Series of Poker championship event. I picked up two kings and made it $300 to go, Jay Heimowitz called, and the flop came:

I bet $400 at the pot and Jay made a big raise of around $3,000. I didn't hesitate in throwing away the kings because I knew that he wouldn't raise me with anything smaller than two aces or a set. Sure enough, he showed me pocket nines.

I knew that because Jay is an excellent player he would not have stood a raise with a hand such as A-J, and that he had to have a pocket pair. The only pairs that I could have beaten on the flop were tens, jacks, or queens. When you're playing against a top player like Jay, he isn't moving in with two jacks, two queens, or even two kings. So, I figured that he either had two aces or a set—he wouldn't have 10-8 or 8-6 for a straight draw. I lost $700 on the hand, but at least I wasn't knocked out of the tournament.

Actually, this was the second time in a row that Jay had flopped top set against an overpair. On the hand just before this one,

Tommy Grimes had two aces and brought it in for about $400, and Jay called the bet. The flop came 10-7-2. Tommy bet $2,000 at the pot and Jay moved in. Tommy made the mistake of calling him. Jay had flopped top set, trip tens, and knocked Tommy out of the tournament.

How you play pocket kings against a rag flop depends, once again, on what you know about your opponents. If I were playing Joe Blow from Idaho, I might give him a little action on this hand, especially if I knew that he was a limit hold'em player. Limit players seem to think that when they have top pair with top kicker or an overpair in no-limit they have the Holy City. A player such as Jay Heimowitz knows that I either have an overpair or am taking a shot with A-K or A-Q (since it was a small flop), and that I am putting him on either the A-K or A-Q, too. But once I bet the flop and he raised it, I knew where he was with the hand.

Why did he make such a huge raise? If he put me on a big overpair, he may have figured that I would play it, but I didn't. He also knew that if he flat called I would shut down if I didn't hit anything, so he may as well try to get me to play the hand on the flop. Also, you never want to give a free card in a tournament. Jay knew that he had the pot won on the flop, so why not take it right then? Why give me a chance to bust him if one of my cards came off on the turn?

46. HOW TO PLAY KINGS AGAINST AN ACE-BOARD

Suppose you are holding two kings in the middle stage of a $1,000 buy-in tournament. Player A has limped into the pot. You raise and he calls. Everyone else folds.

The flop comes:

SCENARIO ONE

Player A checks. What do you do? A lot of players will check their ace on the flop, so you should check too.

SCENARIO TWO

You are in first position with kings and you raised before the flop. Player B called your raise. What do you do when the flop comes with an ace?

Because the ace is on the board, you check. Player B probably also checks—a good player will check his ace on the flop if the raiser has checked in front of him. Suppose the turn comes with the 2♣—in a tournament, you check again.

Player B probably will bet, although he could wait until fifth street. He knows that you don't have an ace and he may try to trap you on the end. But once the ace comes on the flop, you are through with the hand, and will only play it to the showdown for free.

47. HOW TO PLAY TWO KINGS: OVERPAIR

In the middle stage of a big no-limit tournament, you are dealt two kings for the third time. You raise before the flop and one opponent calls. The flop comes:

How do you play your overpair?

SCENARIO ONE

This time, you lead with the kings, thinking that someone at the table holds a hand such as A♠ Q♦ or K♥ Q♥, hands that a player might call a raise with. If one of those hands is out, then you might get a play when you bet, and if the 6♥ comes on the turn you want to make a healthy bet because you don't want to give anybody a chance to make two pair.

SCENARIO TWO

Suppose you're up against a player who stood your pre-flop raise with pocket queens. Some tournament players think that queens are the holy nuts and will even reraise with them. But since nobody reraised before the flop, you go with the kings and then try to shut them out on fourth street with a big bet.

There also is the chance that someone

holds K-J suited and will call your opening bet on a straight draw. Although he probably will call you on the flop, if you put in a big bet at fourth street he will throw away the hand (unless he is a horrible player). In no-limit or pot-limit hold'em, you can freeze out the draws on the turn, whereas in limit hold'em you can't.

48. HOW TO PLAY TWO KINGS AT THE WSOP

Hans "Tuna" Lund and I were faced with this hand at the World Series of Poker. Tuna raised the pot from early position and it was passed all the way to me on the button. I flat-called him with:

The flop came:

Tuna held A-Q and led at the pot. What would you do?

I flat called the bet. On the turn, he led at the pot again. This time, I moved over the top of him and Tuna threw away the hand.

It pays to take a chance once in a while. You hear so many people say, "Every time I have kings, an ace comes on the flop." If an ace comes, so what? Just throw away the hand. In this example, I played to win a big pot, and was able to extricate $2,700 from my opponent. I knew that Tuna likely held A-Q or A-K before the flop, but there was a pretty good chance that I had the best hand, as it was the second-best pair you can be dealt.

In limit, pot-limit, and no-limit hold'em tournaments, it is not unusual for players to raise from early position with hands such as A-Q, A-J, or A-10. I don't suggest raising with A-Q in a full ring, but five-handed or less, I will raise with the hand. At a full table, I think that hands such as A-Q, A-J, or A-10 (suited or unsuited) in the first four seats are very weak, because if you raise with them and get called, where are you? It seems that when you start with the worst hand, you invariably flop a pair to it and then you're stuck in the pot. You try to avoid that situation by not playing these types of hands in early position, especially in a no-limit hold'em tournament.

TWO QUEENS

49. HOW TO PLAY TWO QUEENS

Two queens is sometimes very difficult to play in both no-limit and pot-limit hold'em. It's almost always too good to throw away, but it's also vulnerable against A-K, as well as K-K and A-A. Often, your success in a tournament depends on when you push with queens and when you get away from them, or when you do both.

I was playing at the Bellagio Five-Diamond tournament in 2002, and faced down this situation. The first spot brought it in for a raise of $150. There were four callers to me in the little blind holding two queens. I reraised $1,200, overbetting the pot a little bit—I wanted to win the pot right there, or get only one other player to call me. The big blind called the $1,200 and raised another $4,000. Everybody folded around to me, and I threw the hand away so fast it looked like 3-2. The big blind showed me two kings, but that's beside the point. The point is that if you're not prepared to get away from two queens, you'd better not play no-limit hold'em. Although there are a lot of scenarios where pocket queens is a great hand, there also are a lot of situations where it isn't.

QUEENS IN EARLY POSITION

Do not slow-play queens from a front position because any ace or king that comes on the flop will put you in jeopardy. You want to bring them in for a raise in order to get some money into the pot. In the early stage of the tournament, if a player reraises a substantial portion of his chips before the flop, pocket queens is not the type of hand that you want to take a stand with (or take heat with before the flop). You should release them in this scenario. A smart, timely laydown is just as important as making the right calls and raises.

One play that you do *not* make with pocket queens is playing second-hand low. (Pocket aces is the only hand that you play second-hand low strategy.) The reason why is that when you just call after a couple of limpers have entered the pot, you don't know where you're at with pocket queens.

Suppose you have pocket queens against one opponent and the flop comes J-8-2. You make a bet and get called. You can beat A-J, Q-J, 10-9, and other hands like them. But your opponent could have pocket eights or a straight draw, which would lead him to call you. It's also possible that he slow-played with aces or kings. But still, you can't afford to give a free card when you have queens. If you check, you face the possibility that an ace or king will come on the turn and then you've lost a hand that you should have won.

The only time that you can trap with queens is when you're up against very aggressive players who will bet every time that you check. But overall, never give a free card in tournament poker when you have the best hand.

QUEENS IN LATE POSITION

If you hold queens in late position, or, more importantly, on the button, and a few players have limped in front of you, your queens get more valuable. The chances are that no one behind you (the blinds) has a bigger pair than yours. Always raise with the queens—then if you get a small flop, you can try to win the pot right away.

The major consideration with queens is not what you do with them when you have the best hand, but how you get away from them when you don't.

Although it sounds as though we're telling you to play two queens very cautiously, the fact is that queens is the third-best starting hand in hold'em. Pocket queens increase in value as the number of players at your tournament table decreases. Remember that the lower your pair, there are more and more pairs out there that are higher, and more overcards that can beat you.

POT-LIMIT PLAY

Pocket queens play the same way in pot-limit hold'em as they do in no-limit. Raise the size of the pot before the flop and lead the size of the pot on the flop if you think you have the best hand. It'd be nice to win the pot right there, but if you get called that's okay too. Continue betting the queens as long as you think they are the best hand. Remember that in pot-limit you always raise the full amount of the pot.

TWO JACKS

50. HOW TO PLAY TWO JACKS

Suppose you are sitting in an early position during the early stage of a no-limit, freeze-out tournament, and you have two jacks. Do you bring it in with a raise, or do you just limp?

SCENARIO ONE

My suggestion is that you limp with a pair of jacks (or tens) in this situation. If you raise and get reraised, what are you going to do with the hand? If you don't get raised, you could flop a jack and win a big pot, because nobody will put you on that big a hand to start with. You take the chance, of course, of having a player coming in with something like a little ace or K-Q and beating you. If someone outflops you and wins the hand, you would have been beaten anyway. But by not raising before the flop, you will lose less money if somebody does make a better hand on the flop.

Of course, if you had raised before the flop, they may not have played those little-ace or K-Q hands, but the bigger worry is that you'd getting reraised and forced to throw away the hand when you have money invested in the pot.

SCENARIO TWO

Imagine that you are sitting in fifth position and it has been passed to you. In that case, you should raise with the jacks at any point in the tournament. This situation is very different from scenario one, as now you already have four people out of the pot and there are only four players sitting behind you.

Early in the tournament when the antes are $25-$50, you might raise $150 to $200 with the jacks. In a big buy-in tournament such as the World Series you have $10,000 in front of you, so $200 would be a reasonable raise. You don't make huge raises of $4,000, for example, early in a tournament; instead you make the small raise because you think that you have the best hand before the flop. You are trying to do one of two things: Either win the pot immediately; or get called and win the pot as it develops. After all, the jacks aren't the best hand that you can have, and you couldn't even call with them on a lot of flops.

SCENARIO THREE

Now suppose you are in the late stages of a tournament with the two jacks in your hand. Later in the tournament, you definitely want to raise with two jacks. Say that you are playing at a shorthanded table with six or fewer players. Four tables are left in the tournament and each one of them is shorthanded. In that case you have to play the jacks much stronger than you would earlier, although you don't necessarily want to commit your whole stack with the jacks.

ACE-QUEEN

51. HOW TO PLAY ACE-QUEEN

Ace-queen is a trouble hand that should be played with caution. During the first levels of play in a nine or ten-handed game you don't want to put a lot of money in the pot with A-Q (suited or unsuited) from an early position. Treat a suited hand as a bonus, but something that should not change how you play. Although I prefer suited cards when I play an A-Q, A-J, or A-10, I value their ranks more than whether or not they're suited.

You can't stand a reraise before the flop with A-Q in the opening rounds. If you catch either an ace or a queen on the flop, you will be in a bind as to what to do if someone bets at you. Why put yourself in that situation?

Suppose you flopped a queen and an early position raiser makes a big bet at the pot. Ask yourself what he could have, particularly if he's willing to jeopardize a lot of chips. People won't usually risk going broke early in a tournament unless they have a big pocket pair. In fact, it's easier to play *any* pair from up front than A-Q because a small to medium pair plays so easily after the flop—no set, no bet—whereas an A-Q or A-J require a lot of judgment if you get any action on the flop.

If I'm in middle to late position early in the tournament and there are other limpers in the pot, I'll consider taking a cheap flop with the hand, but I won't raise with it. If there are no limpers, I like to bring it for a modest raise of about three times the size of the big blind. If anyone comes over the top I fold. If I flop top pair, I usually will make a pot-sized bet on the flop, but if I get played with, I usually will shut down.

Later in the tournament, particularly when you're playing at a shorthanded table, A-Q becomes more valuable. When you're either short stacked or are up against a short stack, you might have to take a stand with the hand.

ACE-JACK

52. HOW TO PLAY ACE-JACK

If A-Q is a trouble hand, A-J and A-10 are even more dangerous. These are hands that can take no heat whatsoever before the flop at practically any stage of the tournament.

A-J is a little bit stronger than A-10 because of its higher kicker. A-10 gains some value from the 10—although it's a weak kicker, it can make a straight. As usual, being suited is strictly a bonus. Occasionally you will have to take a stand with these types of hands when, for example, your stack has deteriorated or another player is so short-stacked that he has to play cards that he usually wouldn't.

Generally speaking, these are limping hands from middle to late position when others have entered the pot, and you sometimes can raise with them from late position when no one has entered. But discard them if anyone plays back at you.

KING-QUEEN

53. HOW TO PLAY
KING-QUEEN

In no-limit hold'em K-Q is a trap hand. Unless you flop something like J-10-9, A-J-10, two kings and a queen, or even two pair, you're in dire circumstances with this hand. You especially wouldn't want to play king-queen in a full ring game, and the same can be said for Q-J. In fact, I give a little more value to J-10 because you can make more straights with the hand than you can make with either K-Q or Q-J.

K-Q IN LATE POSITION

Suppose you're playing in a $2,000 tournament and are dealt K-Q. The action is passed to you on the button. How do you play the hand?

In no limit, I treat K-Q like deuce-trey, like it's the plague—unless it's passed to me on the button. Then I might raise the two blinds, but that is the only place that I would raise with it. Although it helps if the K-Q is suited, that still doesn't change the fact that this combination can get you into big trouble.

Now suppose you are on the button with K-Q and a player raises in front of you. What do you do?

I surely would not stand a raise with this hand, or raise with it myself. Let's say you raise with the hand and someone calls you.

The flop comes:

Now, what are you going to do? You have top pair with second kicker. In other words, you don't have anything! There is a good chance that since you were called before the flop, someone who has an A-Q has you beaten already.

K-Q IN THE BLINDS

You are in the little blind with the K-Q. Everybody else has passed. What do you do?

In this case, you can raise the big blind, even though you are out of position and will have to act first after the flop. Some players will call a small raise from the big blind with hands that aren't very good because they already have money in the pot, but the chances are good that you'll win the pot right there with your pre-flop raise.

ACE-WHEEL CARD

54. HOW TO PLAY
ACE-WHEEL CARD

In order to play an ace with a wheel card profitably, the right set of circumstances should be in place. Ace-little suited (or unsuited) is not a hand that you should play from an early position. It's of little value to you from up front because if an ace comes on the flop and you bet it and get played with, you have no kicker. Obviously the best flop for ace-small suited is three to your suit or three wheel cards, but the odds against a flop like that are so great that you will definitely lose a lot of money in the long run if you play ace-small every time you get it.

Now suppose you are in middle to late position and a couple of players have limped in. Since it's developing into a multiway pot, you might limp with it and see the flop cheaply. If you get a good flop in multiway action you have the chance to win a nice pot. You don't want to stand a raise with A-4, and you don't want to play it heads up. So, when you call a limp bet, be prepared to throw it away if someone raises. Folding against a raise should be a part of your thinking even before you limp into the pot.

Suppose you're in the cutoff seat or on the button and no one has entered the pot. Should you raise with ace-small? No, you don't want to put yourself in a situation where you can't get rid of this type of hand before the flop. Personally, I never play this hand aggressively. (In no-limit circles we call it a "sucker hand.") Let's say that you raised on the button and the small blind calls the raise. He probably has an ace or a pocket pair, and almost any kicker that he has with his ace will be higher than your wheel card. If his kicker also is a wheel card, more often than not you're still not the favorite if an ace falls.

You can play ace-small from the last two positions, if no one else has entered the pot. But you don't raise with it, you limp. As I have maintained for years, if the four or five players in front of you don't have a hand, there's a good chance that one or two of the players behind you do. That is why you limp rather than raise with ace-small in late position—you cannot stand a reraise and would have to release the hand. And if you raise and get called, you don't have a hand, and if you want to go further with it, you have to be prepared to bluff unless you catch a flop. Why put yourself in that kind of situation? Your goal is to always be in control.

When you're in the small blind against the big blind only, you have three options: raise, fold, or call. If you just call, you might get yourself into trouble; if you fold, you stay out of trouble; raise, and you might win the pot right there. If you have observed that your opponent usually defends his blind, forget about raising. Instead, consider limping against him. If he is someone who raises all the time, he might raise just because you limped. Depending on the type of player he is, you can reraise him; against a different sort, fold if he raises. What you decide to do depends on the kind of read you put on your opponent.

What about playing hands like A-6, A-7, or A-8? None of these ace-middle-card hands can make a straight—your best result is the nut flush if the hand is suited, or two pair if you hit your kicker. You're just throwing your money away if you play them.

PLAYING A-4 IN POT-LIMIT HOLD'EM

In pot-limit hold'em, ace-small has more value. First of all, when you limp in pot-limit, you can't be raised very much. If it's a multiway pot, I would play the hand even against a raise. For example, two players have limped in, you limp in, and then somebody raises, doubling the size of the pot. If any of the other limpers call, you do the same. If they all pass, you pass as well, because you don't want to play this type of hand heads up. If you call and don't catch a good flop you can just throw it away. Also, you must be disciplined enough to fold if you flop an ace to the hand and an opponent bets into you.

You can play some hands in pot-limit that you can't play in no-limit. In pot-limit hold'em, the value of hands change because you can't be blown out of the pot right away. Pot-limit is a game that was designed so that you can take more flops than in no-limit.

In pot-limit you want to play multiway pots whereas you only want to play one or two opponents in no-limit.

A NO-LIMIT ACE-SMALL-CARD SCENARIO

At the 2002 Hall of Fame tournament in heads-up no-limit action, Howard Lederer held A♦ 4♦. Peter Costa had K-6 offsuit.

The flop came:

Costa bet $30,000 and Lederer raised all-in. "I can't find a reason to lay the hand down," Costa said and called the raise. The turn and river brought Lederer no help, and Costa won the title.

ANOTHER ACE-SMALL-CARD SCENARIO

At the Four Queens Classic in 1996, Doyle Brunson and T.J. Cloutier were playing heads-up for the title in the $5,000 no-limit hold'em event. Holding the A♠ 2♠, T.J. raised a significant amount before the flop. Doyle called with J-9 offsuit.

The flop came:

When Doyle bet with his two pair, T.J. moved all in with top pair and the nut flush draw. Doyle called. The 8♦ came on the turn and the 5♦ came at the river. Doyle won the pot and the championship.

We have illustrated this hand to demonstrate that luck will always factor into poker. You might make the right raise with the best hand, but that doesn't guarantee that you're going to like the result.

TWO TENS

55. HOW TO PLAY TWO TENS

Tens and jacks (closely followed by queens) are two of the most difficult hands to play in no-limit and pot-limit hold'em. Although it's better to have pocket jacks than tens, one advantage of tens is that they are somewhat more likely to make a straight thereby making it less likely that someone else can make one, since you hold two of the tens in your hand. Just remember that if you don't flop a set there are four bigger cards that can beat your tens. So if an overcard hits the flop, you can't play your hand confidently. When you have tens it's likely that one or more overcards will come on the flop, whereas with jacks it's about even money.

If you are the first one in the pot, you can bring it in for a raise. If you are reraised, do not hesitate to throw your tens away. On the other hand, if there's a limper in early position and you're in second position you should be very reluctant to raise, because if you get called and then raised by a player in a later position, you probably don't have the best hand. However, if there is a limper in early position and you're sitting in the last two seats, you definitely can raise with pocket tens. If the limper comes back over the top, you can fold.

Now suppose that you have pocket tens one spot in front of the button (the cutoff seat). You raise and the big blind calls. The board comes:

The big blind checks to you, and after you bet he comes over the top with a reraise. What do you do? You can't possibly like your hand when someone comes over the top of you — either he thinks you're on a steal, or he has a big hand and is trying to suck you in. If you have only a relatively small amount of chips left, you might go with the hand, but if you have a lot of chips, pass or use your own judgement on the hand. There are situations when your opponent might raise with a pair of eights or nines, or A-7, and your knowledge of his play should guide your decision to continue or simply fold and get two new cards on the very next hand.

In other words, be very cautious when you flop an overpair to the board. You can bet, of course, but if someone comes over the top, you can be in a dangerous situation. People like to trap in this situation.

EARLY TO MIDDLE POSITION

From early to middle position you can bring it in for a raise with pocket tens, especially if you're the first one in the pot. Just determine in advance that you aren't going to take any serious heat with the hand. If someone raises behind you, it's usually time to bail out.

You also can limp with pocket tens from early to middle position, whether you are the first one in or one or two limpers are already in the pot. If you get any heat before the flop it's usually a pass. For example, in the early stages of a big buy-in tournament when lots of chips are in play, just calling a minimum bet certainly is a viable strategy. On the flop, you want to hit a set — and if you don't, you can get away from them without losing much money because you only limped before the flop.

LATE POSITION

Suppose you are in late position and only one (or no) limpers have entered the pot after five or six people have passed. In this scenario, you should bring it in for a raise with pocket tens.

There are times in tournaments when you might play tens like you would play deuces — especially in the early stages of a big buy-in tournament when lots of chips are in play and the blinds are small. You don't put a lot of heat on the pot yourself and you don't take any heat to the hand. You might just slip in and hope to flop a set, not getting too involved if you don't.

In the later stages of the tournament you might have to take a stand with your tens because of your chip position. Also, as the table gets shorter (i.e., the number of players is reduced), there is the tendency for more rags to be dealt. Therefore, tens improve in value in shorthanded play. But don't let yourself get lulled to sleep during this stage. A lot of people excuse their faulty play by saying, "Well, I knew he didn't have much of a hand." Remember that it's always possible for someone to have a big hand—I've seen hands dealt three-handed when aces, kings, and queens were out.

You must be prepared to play differently against different opponents in different scenarios. If you aren't willing to tailor your play to the situation, you can get broke to tens (or any other hand) very easily. So even though tens increase in value at a shorthanded table, keep in mind all of these other factors when you play them.

MIDDLE PAIRS

56. HOW TO PLAY MIDDLE PAIRS

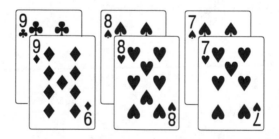

Of course the bigger the pair the better off you are, and the smaller the pair the more vulnerable you are, but for all practical purposes there isn't a lot of difference in the way that you play these middle pairs. Although nines are a little stronger than sevens or eights, and can be played in more or less the same way as tens, the biggest difference it that nines don't give you as good a chance to make a straight, unless a 10 or 5 hits the board. You can't stand much heat with these hands, and you don't want to put much heat on the pot with them either.

Middle pairs should be played very cautiously. You can raise with them from late position if you are the first one in the pot, but be prepared to pitch them if you get played with. If you get called, play them carefully after the flop.

Your chip position often dictates how to play middle pairs. There are times when you are forced to play them — for example, when you're very low on chips and believe that you probably won't get a better hand to play. That's when you take a stand with middle pairs.

SMALL PAIRS

57. HOW TO PLAY SMALL PAIRS (SIXES)

At last, you have made it to the final table in a no-limit hold'em tournament. The table is six-handed and you look down at pocket sixes on the button. The action is passed to you.

A very famous tournament player that I know has a favorite move at the final table of a tournament, and there are lots of players that try to do the same thing. When they are sitting around back with a pair of sixes or fives they invariably move in their whole stack if it is passed to them. I think that this is a horrible play, yet I've seen it happen time and time again: A player loses his entire stack because he moves in all of his chips with a small pair.

When you have worked that hard to get to the final table, why take the chance of losing everything to such a crappy hand? If the first four of five players in front of you don't have anything, there's a decent chance that one of the players behind you *will*.

In this situation, it might be okay to make a small or even decent-sized raise. For example, say that the antes are $200 and the blinds are $400-$800 at a six-handed table. There is $2,400 in the pot, and you have $15,000 in front of you. If you want to raise, why not bring it in for $3,000? That's plenty—if you get reraised or out-flopped, you can get away from the hand. But what are you going to do if you move in your whole stack and get called?

People always talk about the fact that A-K is only an 11 to 10 underdog to a pair. But what they don't realize is that if you have two sixes, and your opponent has 8-7, his hand also is only an 11 to 10 dog to your pair of sixes. It isn't just the A-K that is the underdog: *Any* two overcards are an 11 to 10 underdog to a pair, and if they're suited, they are a slightly smaller dog to the pair. These numbers are what make moving in your whole stack with a small or medium pair such a bad play.

58. HOW TO PLAY SMALL PAIRS (FOURS)

If you're getting three or four callers in a raised pot and you're sitting around back with a lot of chips, obviously it's nice to have pocket fours. But playing heads-up or even a three-way pot isn't a good idea with little pairs.

From a front position, I throw pocket fours away as though it's 7-2. You can only stand a raise with pocket fours if you're getting very good pot odds, and obviously you're hoping to flop a set and rake in a good pot. But if you don't flop a set to your little pair there are very few scenarios where you can play them. In other words, you need to get very lucky to win with small pairs.

Small pairs are takeoff hands in no-limit when you have a lot of chips. Keep in mind that 4-4 is only an 11 to 10 favorite over a 6-5. When you take that into account, there are a lot of hands better than two fours. Pocket fives have a little more value because 5 is a straight card.

Yet time and time again you see players

strapped for chips and clinging to life play these hands: One player has $3,000 in chips, looks down at a baby pair, and moves in everything he's got. If he gets called at most he's an 11 to 10 favorite but he could also be a 4.5 to 1 dog. Of course if you're anteing more than $200 or so, and you have $800 with the blinds coming up, that's a different situation. In that scenario, you might play the hand, but with $3,000 or $4,000 in chips, you have time to wait for a better hand.

While there are certain situations when you can play small pocket pairs, you should usually avoid them. If you stand a little raise in no-limit with a baby pair, it's almost always because you have huge implied odds, lots more chips than the other players, and you're getting multiway action, whereas playing hands like 4-4 heads-up for a raise is almost always a mistake. People who move in with these types of hands are just asking to get broke.

POT-LIMIT NOTES

It's better to play small pairs in pot-limit than in no-limit. You might play a small pair from early position in pot-limit, and you may even stand a small raise with it—so long as you are in decent chip position. The basic difference is that in pot-limit you usually don't have to put as much money in the pot to see a flop as you do in no-limit. Obviously, if you call a raise and get reraised you can always fold without losing too many chips. Do not call raises very often with little pairs in pot-limit or you'll do big damage to your stack. Pick your spots and your opponents carefully.

MIDDLE SUITED CONNECTORS

59. HOW TO PLAY MIDDLE SUITED CONNECTORS

The 9-8 suited is interesting in that it has a lot of potential to be a takeoff hand in the right situations, but it is a chip burner if it is not played properly.

Middle connectors are hands that you play in side games to try to take somebody off. In tournaments, one big drawback is always staring you in the face—you can't go back to your pocket when you lose all your chips.

EARLY POSITION

A 9-8 suited or offsuit is an absolute no-no in early position because it can't stand any pressure. Always remember that the chips you do not lose on bad hands will be available to you later to possibly double or triple up with on your good hands. It's hell to lose a lot of chips on lousy hands, finally wake up with a hand, double up with it, and then find yourself right back where you started, rather than being ahead. You have to think about all these things in tournament play—and especially when you're thinking about playing hands such as 9-8, 8-7, or 7-6 suited from up front.

If you think of playing middle connectors in no-limit hold'em like you would play them in Omaha, you know that any time you flop nothing more than an open-ended straight draw, you don't bet it. If you had other outs in addition to the straight, you might call a bet. If you implant this same kind of thinking in your head when you happen to play middle connectors in no-limit hold'em and flop to them, you'll remember that if you get played with, somebody probably has a draw-out hand.

You want to play small pots with middle

suited connectors. Stay away from big pots, which means that you shouldn't lead with drawing hands unless you're prepared to stand a raise, as in the example above where you have a straight draw, a flush draw, and two overcards to the board. You also can lead if you happen to flop a straight, two pair, or a set. Play it strong if a good card comes for you on fourth street, but don't get involved early. Give yourself a chance to get away from the hand.

LATE POSITION

When two or more limpers have entered the pot, you might occasionally play middle connectors from the cutoff seat or the button.

If everyone passes to you on the button and you have the 9♥ 8♥ you have to fold. Remember that if nobody in front of you has a hand, somebody behind you might. McEvoy calls it the "bunching factor," meaning that if no one has big cards in front, it is somewhat more likely that big cards are bunched behind. Some people like to limp with middle connectors in this situation, but what are you trying to accomplish when you do that? If nobody has called before you and you limp from the cutoff seat or the button, where is the value in the hand? If either the button or the small blind call, you could be a big dog in the hand. And if only the big blind plays, even if he only holds a hand as weak as 10-2 offsuit, he's still a favorite over you.

Now suppose you have 9-8 in the small blind and everybody has passed. Naturally, you call for one-half a bet. If you get raised, you throw the hand away.

The only time that I see value in middle-connector hands such as 9♣ 8♣ in no-limit is when you hold them in the big blind in an unraised pot, or when you call for one half-bet from the small blind. If the flop comes 9 high, you're not going to play aggressively. Remember that there are a lot of people who play ace-anything—A-9, A-10, A-8—for the minimum bet.

Just because any two cards can win in poker, it doesn't mean that you should play them.

POT LIMIT NOTES

The value of 9-8 goes up somewhat in pot-limit hold'em because when you're raised in pot-limit, the raise is smaller than it would be in no-limit. Sometimes, then, you can call a raise with middle connectors because you're getting the right price for it, and if you flop good to the hand, you might get paid off pretty good. Certainly middle connectors are not as big chip burners as they are in no-limit. In no-limit, the hand might cost you $300 to play at the first level, whereas it might cost you only $85 in pot-limit. Like any other hand, the price must be right to justify playing this type of hand.

THE "7-2" FACTOR

60. HOW TO PLAY THE "7-2" FACTOR

Let's take a look at a tournament situation in which you don't have a "hand," just two useless cards. Years ago at the Queens Classic we were playing nine-handed at the final table. The antes were $500 and the blinds were $3,000-$6,000. Sitting in the big blind, I had a total of $13,000 in chips before I posted the $6,000 big blind and $500 ante. The next hand was going to cost me $3,500 more. Looking down at my cards, I had 7-2 offsuit. The hand was passed around to the button, who raised. The little blind threw his hand away, and the action was up to me. I did not hesitate to call for one reason — I knew that if the button had ace-something or king-something, so long as he wasn't paired, I was only a 2 to 1 dog. However, for the size of the pot, my odds weren't quite as good, so I called. He had A-J, I paired the deuce, won the pot, and went on to win second place.

The point of this story is that you can never let yourself get so low in chips that even if you double up you still won't have any chips to play with. In some tournament situations you have to play any two cards. You sometimes are better off going in with a nothing-hand than you would be if you anted off your last chips. There's always the chance that you can win the pot without a fight or out-flop your opponent.

We call this type of scenario the "7-2 Factor." Sometimes a tournament situation will dictate literally playing any two cards — we use 7-2 as an example because it generally is considered to be the worst possible starting hand in hold'em. In other words, you sometimes will have to take a stand with a 7-2 type of hand because the alternative is even less appetizing.

If I had thrown the hand away, I would have had $6,500 left with $3,500 of it going in for the ante and the small blind in the very next pot. Now suppose I didn't catch a playable hand in the small blind—I would have to quadruple my chips just to get back the money that I had before I went through the two blinds. The point is that you are better off making a move before you get yourself into that kind of situation.

Your fate is practically sealed anyway—if you call and lose, you didn't have enough chips to play in any case, and if you fold, you still don't have any chips. So why not give yourself at least some chance of winning? By calling, you're simply making the best of a bad situation.

BUILD YOUR STACK

by Tom McEvoy

61. HOW TO BUILD YOUR STACK

I recently played in a major tournament in which the chip leader going into the final table outdistanced his nearest competitor by a 5 to 1 margin—and blew it, finishing in sixth place. You've seen the same kind of thing happen yourself, haven't you? The favorite loses the race to a dark horse when he makes a fatal error or loses a few key hands, or doesn't use common sense in managing his stack.

In a tournament, your stack is your most precious asset. You work hard to build it, like you'd build your dream house. An architect designs a blueprint before he builds, and you must design a tournament game plan to build a competitive war chest. Your building blocks are chips; the more of them you have, the stronger your foundation. In most tournaments, you try to build your stack by about 25 percent during each round in the early and middle stages, and you hope to double up in the later stages. In games like Omaha high-low split, you accumulate chips slowly, whereas in no-limit or pot-limit hold'em, you can double or triple your stack in one hand. The old saying, "It takes money to make money" is true of chips too. A big stack is very intimidating at all stages of a tournament, so that it takes greater strength in your opponents' hands for them to compete against you when you have a tower of chips.

You also need a backup plan for when you suffer big beats. For example, how will you handle things if you get a big hand snapped off, leaving you short-stacked? Your plan should include what to do in other stressful situation (like going all in to call a big raise) and how to play different opponents. You've got to get into your opponents' heads to get some insight into their playing style, which hands they raise with, what kinds of hands they are likely to bluff with, and so on.

Some players try to win tournaments too early by attempting to accumulate big stacks of chips in the first round or two. Usually this simply is not going to happen. If you can double up in the first round, you've done a marvelous job, and adding even 50 percent to your stack is an achievement. But it is unrealistic to believe that you can amass three to four times your original stack after only one round of play, unless you catch a tremendous rush of cards.

When you are short-stacked late in the tournament, you frequently will have to take a stand with less than a premium hand. The shorter your stack, the more important it is to use good judgment about when to jeopardize it. This is especially true when you have only one or two bets left, because you know that you will be called by at least the big blind, if not someone with a bigger collection of chips. So you have to wait and then take your best shot. You don't necessarily have to wait for A-K, but you also don't want to risk your chips by going all in with 10-9 or K-7, if you can help it.

With a big stack late in the tournament, you should attack the short stacks at every opportunity. The more chips you have, the more your options, but even with a massive amount of chips you still have to use good judgment, especially in deciding whether to go up against other big stacks. You have to wait for premium hands before you attack one of the other big boys.

You also can capitalize on the tight play of your opponents by betting more aggressively when they don't have much to play with. Even though they may suspect that you are raising with less than a premium hand, there isn't much that they can do about it if they have an average hand. Big stacks are weapons—use them!

At the final two or three tables, I take a cruise around to see how many short stacks there are, and how many more players need to be eliminated before I can make it to the final table. Sometimes this census affects my playing strategy. For example, if I am on a short stack and I see a couple of other players who have even less, I wait for a prime hand before betting big—especially if the other short stacks are about to get eaten up by the blinds. Of course I won't throw away aces or kings, because I don't just need enough chips to survive, but enough to go all the way. Never lose sight of the big picture—winning the tournament. But knowing the chip counts of the guys at the other tables, the short stacks in particular, is definitely useful.

One of the trickiest tournament skills is playing a mid-sized stack. In many situations, you will be doing more check-calling with a mid-sized stack. Suppose you entered the pot in late position with K-J and flopped a king, the highest upcard. If there are connecting cards that look dangerous, you could easily run into two pair or a straight draw. Although you may have been leading at the pot, if the river card is a connector that could make two pair or a straight for someone else, you should check-call if it looks like you still have the best hand. Even if you may bet the pot in a side game, it's better to play more conservatively in a tournament, and check-calling is usually the way to go. It also may induce a bluff on the end from a player whose hand did not materialize.

Always be aware of your stack status and what round of the tournament you are in. In the early to middle rounds, chips begin to get redistributed and you need to know who has the taller stacks and who has the shorter ones, and where your stack stands in relation to theirs.

Unfortunately, it's not as easy to build a stack as it is to blow it. You can be sure that the players you're going to read about in the next section knew how to build their stacks to get to the money table—even if a few of them blew their chips after they got there or suffered bad beats on good hands that robbed them of victory. In either case, their stories are instructional and interesting if for no other reason than that they got there.

KEY CONCEPTS LEARNED AT THE WORLD SERIES OF POKER

I

INTRODUCTION

Key hands are the ones that turn the tide of fortune during a poker tournament. Few players realize that the key hand in a tournament might well be played long before the final table. If you win your key hands, you're in good shape; if you lose them, you probably will be out of action early. For example, the key hand at the 1984 World Series of Poker championship event was not the last hand played between Jack Keller, the winner, and Cowboy Wolford, the runner-up. In fact, Keller wasn't even involved in the key hand that led him to victory, it was played between Wolford and Jesse Alto, who finished third. And when Jack Straus defeated Dewey Tomko in 1982 when he rivered the winning card, it actually was a previous hand that Straus had played and lost, leaving him with only one chip, that led him to eventual victory.

Spectators are often amazed that the winning hand at the final table is so weak. But seasoned tournament veterans understand that in heads-up play, it doesn't take a strong hand to win a showdown—it only takes the best hand, as Doyle Brunson wrote years ago. Brunson is proof positive of this axiom—he won the championship two years in a row with a lowly 10-2 (a "Brunson," in poker parlance).

For most of the key hands described, we watched tapes of final-table action at the WSOP. For some we relied upon written reports, and for others we were there to see them. For a precious few, we wrote from personal experience—T.J. has been there four times and I have been there once. These are the hands of destiny.

WSOP CONCEPTS FROM 1978

1. HOW TO BLUFF AND TURN THE TIDE

1978 WSOP FINAL TABLE
Bobby Baldwin versus Crandall Addington
by T.J. Cloutier

When he was about 28 years old, Bobby Baldwin was considered to be the best no-limit hold'em player alive. He was very highly regarded by a lot of people, by all the old pros. Bobby Hoff once said that Baldwin was 15 percent better than anybody playing at that time. During the 1978 World Series of Poker, Baldwin and Crandall Addington were playing heads-up for the title when Baldwin pulled off a successful bluff that changed the entire course of the tournament. Although it was not the final hand, it was the key hand because it shifted the momentum of the final-table play.

Addington had the lead at this point. With the blinds at $3,000-$6,000, he raised $10,000. We don't know what his cards were, but we do know that Baldwin called the raise with 10-9 offsuit. People don't realize that a lot of times, hands are played before the players ever see a flop. When Baldwin called Addington's raise, he probably had already decided that even if he didn't get a great flop he was going to win the pot anyway. In other words, long before the flop actually came up, Baldwin knew he was going to make a move.

The flop came Q-3-4 with two diamonds, and Baldwin led at it for a substantial amount, which Addington called. Off came the ace of diamonds on the turn, putting three diamonds on the board, and Baldwin moved in. That was his opportunity. You've heard me say a million times that you must have nerves of iron to play no-limit hold'em—you have to be willing to sacrifice everything you have on a major bluff. And Baldwin was such a good player that he didn't think twice about it. When the board came with something that he could represent, even though Addington had called him on the flop, Baldwin moved on it.

What if the turn card had been a brick? In that case Baldwin would have shut down. He would have taken his loss with the hand because he knew that Addington had something when he called him on the flop. Baldwin also understood that when he moved in on the turn Addington could have had two diamonds in his hand, but that was the chance he had to take. Since Addington had raised before the flop he could have had a pair or a "big ace" instead of two diamonds, in which case Baldwin's power play would work. When an ace came on the turn, if Addington had put Baldwin on a flush, he wouldn't have called anyway even if he had a big ace—but he would've taken more time to muck his hand. As it happened, he threw his cards away quickly, so the chances are that he did not have a big ace. Baldwin flashed his cards as he scooped in the pot, but we'll never know what Addington had.

The bluff changed the tide at the final table. If Addington had called, with, for example, a queen, the tournament would have been over because Baldwin probably had no outs, and Addington would have had what he coveted more in life than all the money that he had earned from the oil business: which was very substantial. He would have won the World Series of Poker.

2. HOW TO GET POT-COMMITTED

1978 WSOP FIVE-HANDED
Jesse Alto versus Louis Hunsucker
by Tom McEvoy

A hand came up at the final table of the 1978 World Series of Poker between Jesse Alto and Louis "Sager" Hunsucker that is a good example of what sometimes happens, especially in no-limit hold'em tournaments, when a player who is bluffing or semi-bluffing calls a raise because the odds give him enough room to justify making the call. In other words, he gets pot-committed.

Hunsucker brought it in for a substantial raise with Q-10 and Alto reraised all in. Hunsucker would have to commit most of his remaining chips—he already had one-half of his chips in the pot—with what he knew probably was the worst hand. He tells Alto that he knows he has the worst hand with only Q-10, thought about it, and finally called. He said that since he already had half his chips in the pot, the odds on his money for putting the rest of his chips in were at a point that he had to go with the hand. "I'm not sure that I would've done it," T.J. Cloutier commented, "but I'm not so sure that I wouldn't have done it either. In those days, it wasn't like you were playing for a million, although they were playing for decent money. So Hunsucker decided to play it."

When they turned over their hands, Hunsucker found himself up against something he certainly did not want to see, Alto's A-Q. There's more drama to it: The flop came queen-high with connecting straight cards on board. Hunsucker needed to either hit a 10 to make two pair, or hit a gutshot straight card on the river to make a straight with the 10 in his hand. The straight card came and Hunsucker won the pot, sending Alto out in fifth place for a payday of $21,000. Hunsucker hung on for third place and pocketed $63,000.

WSOP CONCEPTS FROM 1979

3. SET OVER SET

1979 WSOP EIGHT-HANDED
Bobby Baldwin versus Sam Moon

Eight-handed at the final table, Sam Moon raised with two aces before the flop and was called by three other players, making it a four-way pot. Bobby Baldwin, the defending world champion, saw the flop with pocket eights. The flop came with something like 8-6-3. Baldwin had flopped top set against Moon's aces. Moon bet $30,000 on the flop. Baldwin had $45,000 in front of him and moved in with the rest of his chips. The other two players folded, but Moon called the raise.

There was well over $100,000 in the pot. There were 54 players in the tournament that year and a total of $540,000 in chips in play, meaning that whoever won this pot would become the chip leader. On fourth street Moon spiked an ace and sent Baldwin home in eighth place. So, instead of taking the lead on this hand, Baldwin finished out of the money, as only five places were paid in 1979. This story shows how tough it is for a champion to repeat.

4. GETTING FLUSHED OUT AT THE RIVER

1979 WSOP HEADS UP
Hal Fowler versus Bobby Hoff

Before this key hand unraveled, Bobby Hoff had a 3 to 2 chip lead on Hal Fowler. Hoff had a little over $300,00 and Fowler had a little more than $200,000 of the $540,000 chips in play. Hoff had the K♦ 6♦ on the button and Fowler held the A♦ 8♦. Hoff raised before the flop and Fowler called. The flop came 9♣ J♥ 7♦ The flop gave Hoff nothing except an overcard and it gave Fowler an inside-straight draw. Fowler checked the flop, Hoff led with a $25,000 bet, and Fowler called, drawing to his inside straight and a three-flush with an ace overcard. "We called Fowler, 'Mr. Inside Straight' at this World Series," T.J. commented, "because he consistently drew to inside straights at the final table in particular and made an amazing number of them."

The 2♦ came on fourth street giving both Fowler and Hoff a backdoor flush draw. Fowler checked and Hoff put in a reasonable $30,000. Without hesitating, Fowler called with his middle-buster straight draw, an overcard, and the nut flush draw—a big draw with one card to come.

The river card was the Q♦, which made the flush for both of them. This time Fowler did not check—he moved in with his remaining $144,000. Hoff studied the situation, hesitating for a while—although that may have been more for the audience's benefit than anything else. At this point there was $298,000 in the pot. Hoff had backdoored the second-nuts and thought that he had the winner, so naturally he called the bet.

Surprisingly, Fowler checked the hand twice and then led with it for all his chips. You would think that once he had made the nuts he would have checked to him, if he figured that Hoff would bet. Hoff, the chip leader, acted aggressively, and was kind of out on a limb—he had started by trying to steal the pot and wound up making the hand, only to get it cracked. This hand actually turned the World Series championship event around and put Fowler in the lead for the rest of the tournament.

There were 54 players in this tournament. If they were giving odds on the favorite, who was even-money to take the championship, Fowler would have been 54 to 1 to win it, the longest shot in the whole tournament. And now he had the chip lead at the final table heads-up, which just shows that anybody can do it. On the videotape, Hal said that he had been playing poker for 42 years and had played hold'em for eight years. Although he was an amateur tournament player, at least he understood the basics of the game—and got lucky.

5. HOLDING POCKET ACES AGAINST A DRAW

1979 WSOP FINAL HAND
Hal Fowler versus Bobby Hoff Heads-Up

The final hand at the 1979 World Series of Poker was a classic. Bobby Hoff had $121,000 and Hal Fowler had $419,000. Holding pocket aces, Hoff raised, making it $38,000 to play.

Most players in Fowler's situation—he had a 4 to 1 lead—would look for a premium hand to try to grind a man out in this spot, and he certainly would not play a pot with a weak hand when the other man had raised. But Hal didn't play it that way—he called the raise with 7-6 offsuit, making it a $76,000 pot. Although that is not how most professionals would play when they had a big chip lead, being the amateur that he claimed to be, Hal played any two cards.

The flop came J-5-3. Bobby bet $40,000 and Hal called with an inside-straight draw. Since he had called $38,000 before the flop, it seemed a cinch that he was going to call $40,000 on the flop with a middle-buster straight draw and the chip lead. It's rare that you would even get a flop that gives you something to draw to with 7-6 offsuit. But now Fowler had a chance to bust Hoff if he caught the right card. Of course, off came a four on fourth street. He checked and Hoff bet $43,000 all-in. Naturally, Fowler called—he had made the nuts—and sent Hoff and his pocket rockets to the rail in second place.

Hoff probably would have won the pot if he had been playing against a better, more experienced player because with a lead that big, a world-class player would not have played with him. If you have a 4 to 1 lead on somebody, you don't want to play big pots; instead, all you want is to grind them out. Why give the other guy a chance to catch up? If you have $400,000 and he has $100,000, why would you want to let your lead drop to 3 to 2, meaning that if you lose one pot you will be behind?

Although Fowler didn't understand tournament strategy, he knew how to play the hand once he called, so he was no rank amateur. Once he picked up the draw, he knew that Hoff couldn't break him, so he called $40,000 on the flop to make the straight. Then he was smart enough to check it on the turn. But it didn't matter whether he checked or bet because Hoff was going to call anyway if Fowler led at the pot. His reaction when he won the title was amazing—he just sat there like a mannequin. One commentator attributed his lack of enthusiasm to the apparently large number of Valiums or Qualudes he had consumed to calm his nerves.

WSOP CONCEPTS FROM 1981

6. SET OVER SET TURNS THE TIDE

1981 WSOP SEVEN-HANDED
Perry Green versus Bobby Baldwin

For the third time in four years, Bobby Baldwin made it to the final table. And then, with seven players left in action, he played a key hand against Perry Green that put Green in the position to eventually go to battle heads-up against Stu Ungar for the title.

Here's how it happened: Baldwin was dealt the 9♣ 9♥ and Green had the Q♣ Q♦; the flop came 9♠ 4♥ 3♣. Baldwin flopped top set and checked it to Green, who bet $40,000.

Baldwin then raised $86,000, enough to put Green all-in if he called the raise. Green agonized over the decision, finally making the call with his overpair. When the hands were turned up, Green realized that he was reduced to two outs. A very strong player, Baldwin still had chips left and if he won the hand, he would be the chip leader at the final table.

The J♥ came on the turn, and the Q♥ on the river, giving Green the pot with set over set. Green went nuts after he hit the two-outer on the river, jumping up and down with joy. Now very low on chips, Baldwin just sat there with a weak smile on his face realizing that the hand had put Green in position to win the tournament.

This hand demonstrates the highs and the lows of tournament poker. When Green saw that he was up against Baldwin's three nines, he probably thought, "Oh, God, I've played all this time and now I'm through." And then when the queen hit, his emotions changed entirely. Suddenly everybody was congratulating him. The ebbs and flows in poker definitely can raise your spirits from the pits to the pinnacle, and vice versa.

7. THREE-HANDED WITH KINGS

1981 WSOP THREE-HANDED
Perry Green, Gene Fisher, And Stu Ungar

When it got to three-handed play at the final table, Perry Green had a substantial chip lead, Stu Ungar was a solid second, and Gene Fisher was trailing as a distant third. There were 75 players that year with $750,000 in chips in play.

Green was on the button holding A♠ Q♦ and opened the pot for $80,000 — clearly he overbet. Sitting on $200,000, Stu Ungar called the $80,000 and raised $120,000 more with K♠ K♥, going all-in. Green didn't hesitate very long before calling, although if he hadn't overbet the pot to start with, there's a chance that he might have considered backing off. If Green won the pot, he probably would have 90 percent of the chips, leaving him heads up with Fisher. If Ungar won, Green would still be a solid second in chips, but Ungar would have over half the chips in play, making him the leader.

With all the money in before the flop and the hands turned up, the flop came A♣ 5♦ 10♦. Perry flopped an ace, which reduced

Ungar to two outs to win the hand. He caught one of them on fourth street, the K♦, giving him trip kings. However, Green had flush and inside-straight draws, so he had some redraws to the nuts. The river card was the 4♣, and Ungar took the pot. Winning the hand was the turning point for Stu, as it gave him the lead. If Ungar hadn't won this one—after the ace flopped, he became a big dog to the hand—he couldn't have won the tournament.

8. FLUSH DRAWS HEAD-UP

1981 WSOP HEADS-UP
Stu Ungar versus Perry Green

Another interesting hand came up when Green and Ungar played heads up. The lead had seesawed back and forth several times, which was one of the fascinating things about this final table, and Green had the advantage going into this remarkable hand. Perry was a very aggressive player, as was Stu, and both these guys put in all their money on either premium or drawing hands.

In this hand, Perry got involved with the 10♣ 2♣ on the button against Stu's A♣ J♣. The flop came J♦ 9♣ 8♣. Stu flopped top pair with the nut flush draw, and Perry flopped a flush draw plus an open-ended straight draw.

On the flop they went to war raising back and forth, and finally Perry moved in on Stu. If Perry wins this hand, the tournament is over; if Stu wins he's got a substantial chip lead. There was $554,000 in the pot, out of $750,000 chips in play, to that point the biggest pot ever played during a WSOP tournament.

The fact that Perry gambled so brazenly in this spot is interesting: He could've just called Stu's bet and tried to make his hand cheaply, but instead he decided to go to war right on the flop, and Stu decided not to lay down top pair and the nut flush draw. The J♠ came on the turn, giving Stu trip jacks. When the 6♦ came on the river, Stu won the pot and took the chip lead, although Perry rallied to make another comeback.

9. DRAW AGAINST DRAW AGAINST LUCK

1981 WSOP FINAL HAND
Stu Ungar versus Perry Green

In the very last hand of the tournament, Green and Ungar went to the center with draws. The blinds were $4,000-$8,000. On the button with 10♣ 9♦, Green made it $16,000 to go, a modest raise. Ungar looked down at the A♥ Q♥ and reraised $25,000 more. Green called the raise (a very marginal call), and the flop came 8♥ 7♦ 4♥, giving Ungar the nut flush draw and Green an open-ended straight draw and two overcards. Ungar went for the kill—he bet $100,000. Green called with his last $78,000 in chips. The way the betting went was rather interesting. Without hesitation, Stu moved in—and Green called immediately. The pot had well over $200,000 in it, which was close to one-third of the total chips in play. If Green had won the pot, it would have put him back into a more competitive position, although he still would not have the lead. The turn card was the 4♣, which paired the board but didn't help either one of them. The Q♦ came at the river, pairing Ungar's hand, although it didn't matter because he would've won anyway with ace-high.

Ungar and Green played three key hands against each other in the tournament, and Stu won each of them: Ungar's K-K against Green's A-Q when an ace flopped and a king came on the turn; Ungar's A♣ J♣ against Green's 10♣ 2♣; and the final hand. Green, however, was incredibly lucky against the other players. When he hit a two-out bigger set against Baldwin's set, Green would have been eliminated if Baldwin had won the pot and Baldwin would have become the chip leader.

Thus, the entire course of the tournament was affected. Ungar was lucky to win his hands against Green, and Green was lucky to beat some of the other players to even get that far. Skill and luck is a powerful combination.

WSOP CONCEPTS FROM 1982

10. THE MIRACLE CHIP

1982 WSOP FINAL HAND
Jack Straus versus Dewey Tomko
by Dana Smith

The river card can pack a brutal blow or be a thing of beauty when all the chips are in the center with only one card to come. Before the final-table confrontation between Jack Straus and Dewey Tomko in 1982, Straus had made an error that later actually rescued him. In a hand that has become a part of poker lore, Straus made what he thought was an all-in bet at the pot. His opponent called and won the pot. As he was getting up to leave the table,

Straus discovered that he had overlooked a $500 chip that was partly concealed under the cushioned rim of the table. Since he had not announced his intention to go all in, that lone chip was still in play in what turned out to be a most unlikely key hand. What Straus did with one chip was amazing—he turned a toothpick into a lumberyard and won the championship. The old saying "a chip and a chair" proved itself in dramatic fashion.

In the final hand, Straus and Tomko got all the money in before the flop. Straus had an A-10 offsuit and Tomko held the A♦ 4♦. When a 4 came on the flop, Tomko took the lead only to see it get torpedoed by the river-card, a 10.

In a deja-vu finale nineteen years later, Tomko again sent all his chips to the center, this time with pocket aces, but Carlos Mortensen sank Tomko's ship of dreams when a 9 came at the river to give Mortensen a straight and the 2001 championship of poker. Certainly the river card has not been kind to Tomko, one of the finest players on the tournament circuit.

WSOP CONCEPTS FROM 1983

11. SET AGAINST DRAW

1983 WSOP THREE-HANDED
Doyle Brunson versus Rod Peate
by Tom McEvoy

In 1983 the legendary Doyle Brunson, who already had won back-to-back championships in 1976-1977 and was, with the possible exception of Amarillo Slim, the most famous poker player in the world, finished in third place behind Rod Peate and I. When it was three-handed, Doyle played a hand against Rod Peate and got himself broke. Doyle had the J♦ 9♦ in the small blind. Rod raised on the button with two nines and I folded. The flop

269

came nine-high with two diamonds, giving Doyle top pair and a flush draw—which looks pretty good on the surface—but he was up against Rod's set of nines.

On the flop Doyle checked and Rod bet around $15,000. Doyle moved all in with over a quarter-million in chips, overbetting the pot, apparently trying to run over Rod. But Rod had made it something like $9,000 before the flop, and had made it $15,000 to go on the flop, so he wasn't about to relinquish the hand. He called Doyle's all-in bet and sent the legend to the rail when no diamond came to rescue him.

12. HEADS UP FOR SEVEN HOURS

1983 WSOP HEADS-UP
Tom McEvoy versus Rod Peate
by Tom McEvoy

Rod Peate and I had been playing heads-up for seven hours when the final hand came up. The blinds were $8,000-$16,000 and Rod raised $40,000 on the button with K-J suited. I hadn't gotten one big pocket-pair all day long, and here I was looking down at two queens. "I'm all-in!" I announced. Everybody sensed that the end was finally near.

Rod didn't take a lot of time to call, which surprised me. In hindsight, of course, he regrets his hasty decision, but at the time he was exhausted. I had been playing to try to wear him down and, basically, that plan worked. I think that he just snapped. His rationale in calling my all-in bet probably was, "What if Tom has something like two nines? I still have two overcards."

The flop came 6-6-3. Rod hit a jack on the turn, giving him jacks and sixes. The river card was another three. Rod would have regained the lead if he had been able to draw out on my queens (the pot was over $600,000), although that didn't necessarily mean that he would have won the tournament. When my two queens held up, I jumped up from my seat with my arms raised in victory—it was the thrill of my life.

Rod and I also made World Series history in that we were the first satellite winners to appear at the championship table.

WSOP CONCEPTS FROM 1984

13. MAKING A DRAMATIC BLUFF

1984 WSOP THREE-HANDED
Cowboy Wolford versus Jesse Alto
by Dana Smith

Byron "Cowboy" Wolford pulled off one of the most dramatic bluffs in World Series history at the final table of the 1984 championship event. Few people remember the final hand that Keller and Wolford played for the title, but almost every tournament aficionado remembers this key hand.

The action was down to three players, Cowboy Wolford, Jack Keller, and Jesse Alto (who had the chip lead), when this hand came up. Before the flop, Keller folded on the button, Wolford flat-called from the small blind and Alto checked in the big blind.

The flop came A♣ 9♣ K♦. Wolford bet $15,000 and Alto called. When the K♥ came on the turn, Wolford sent $40,000 into the pot, and again Alto called. The 2♥ came at the river. This time Wolford pushed in all his chips, about $101,000. Alto thought for a long time before finally folding his hand face down, so we don't know what he had. The chances are good, however, that he had a better hand than Wolford's 5-3, which the Texas cowboy flashed.

This key hand changed the fortunes of the three finalists. Apparently on tilt from succumbing to Wolford's start-to-finish bluff, Alto then threw off the rest of his stack to Jack Keller, the eventual champion, promoting Wolford to second place and demoting himself to third. Keeping a cool head at the final table is always a good idea.

The 1984 World Series was unique in that it was the only year that they played with actual money. The chips were exchanged for cash at the final table when it got down to three players, and bills wrapped in $50,000 bundles rolled across the table as they bet back and forth.

WSOP CONCEPTS FROM 1985

14. A KEY HAND IN THE FINAL TABLE

1985 WSOP FINAL TABLE
T.J. Cloutier versus Bill Smith
by T.J. Cloutier

When Bill Smith, Berry Johnston, and I played three-handed at the final table, I got very lucky against Berry in a key hand. Berry raised the pot with A-K offsuit and I called with the A♥ J♥. When the board came K-J-2, Berry bet and I called with second-best pair. Then, on the turn, off came another jack! I finally got lucky against someone at the final table. And that's how Berry went out in third place.

Bill Smith and I used to play the Southern Circuit and we had been close friends for years. Everybody knows that Bill was an alcoholic, and by the time we got to heads-up play, he was just starting to feel the booze. You could always tell when Bill was drunk because he would start calling the flop. If it came 10-7-4, he would say, "21!" And if he had to leave the table for a bathroom break, he'd have a little hop in his step. We used to call it a git-up in his git-along.

When Bill and I started heads-up play, I had the most chips. Then a key hand came up in which I had two nines and he had two kings. I raised and he reraised. Bill won the pot and took a big lead. I started chipping away at him and got to the point where I had one-quarter of the chips and he had three-quarters—Bill was drinking heavily and that made it easy to take the pots. When he was sober, he was the tightest player in the world; when he was half-drunk, he might've been the best player in the world; and when he was drunk, he was horrible.

I had just won a pot with something like a 5-4 suited, and then I looked down at an ace. Bill raised it and I just moved my whole stack in. I didn't even look at my second card because there was a chance that I could win it with a raise, or if not, I'd probably have the best hand anyway, two overcards if he had a small pair. My chances were pretty good.

Bill called my all-in bet and turned over a pair of threes. I looked at my kicker for the first time—it was a 3! I only had one overcard against his pair. The flop came 4-5-10, so I could have caught an ace or a deuce after the flop to make a straight. But I didn't catch anything and Bill won the title.

WSOP CONCEPTS FROM 1987

15. OVERBETTING THE POT LOSES THE BATTLE

1987 WSOP THREE-HANDED
Johnny Chan versus Bob Ciaffone

The hand that gave eventual winner Johnny Chan the lead for good came down when it was three-handed. At that time Bob Ciaffone was in the lead, Chan was second, and Frank Henderson was a distant third. Basically, Ciaffone overbet the pot twice (meaning that the blinds were relatively small relative to the size of his bets) and got himself in over his head when he decided to gamble to draw out.

This is how the play went down: With

the ante at $2,000 and the blinds at $10,000-$20,000, Ciaffone picked up the A♦ 4♦ in the big blind. Chan called on the button with the K♥ Q♥ and Henderson called from the small blind. Ciaffone then raised $85,000 more, overbetting the pot. To Ciaffone's surprise, Chan called. Henderson passed.

The flop came K♣ J♥ 4♣, giving Chan top pair and Ciaffone bottom pair. Ciaffone led at the pot for $185,000, his second overbet, and Chan moved all in with a $240,000 raise. With two face cards on board, Ciaffone had to figure that Chan had caught a piece of the flop. After a long deliberation, he called. "It seemed remote that Chan would be on a draw," Ciaffone wrote in his excellent book, *Pot-Limit & No-Limit Poker*, "but it looked like an ace or a 4 would win the pot for me, and make me a huge favorite to become the World Champion. Since I was almost getting the right odds, and would still be in the hunt if I lost the pot, I called the raise." With no help on the turn or river, Ciaffone lost the pot and Chan took the lead.

Admittedly, Ciaffone did not want to play Chan heads-up, which is probably why he overbet the pot on the flop, to try to get Chan to lay down the hand. He could've still folded, of course, when Chan came over the top of him. "I should have checked that flop,"

Ciaffone wrote in retrospect, "but it only takes one mistake to cost you a tournament — and the title of World Champion. Even so, my experiences at the final table were the greatest thrill in my life."

Later on, Ciaffone went broke with the 7♠ 5♠ when he flopped middle pair and a flush draw against Chan's top pair-top kicker. Chan had A-J and the flop came jack high.

Henderson, who was in last place with 24 players left and came to the final table dead last in chips, slowly climbed the money ladder and finished second to Chan by playing what appears to have been a sound survival strategy. Someday we'll have to find out exactly how he did it!

WSOP CONCEPTS FROM 1988

16. AT A TOUGH FINAL TABLE

1988 WSOP FIVE-HANDED
T.J. Cloutier versus Humberto Brenes
by T.J. Cloutier

Three years after finishing second to Bill Smith in the "Big One," I made the final table for the second time. I thought this was one of the finest tournaments ever, and the final table was a very tough one. Strangely, every time it was passed to Humberto Brenes on the button, he moved in and I was always in the big blind. "Sooner or later, I'm gonna pick up a hand," I thought to myself.

The next time Humberto—who had less

chips than I did—moved all-in on the button, the little blind passed, and I called with A♠ Q♠ in the big blind. In the stands, his Costa Rican friends were asking him what he had. "Nuevo-six," he answered. I knew how to count in Spanish, so I knew that he had a 9-6. Obviously, he was bluffing, just as I thought. The flop was 9-6-x, another 9 came on fourth street, and finally a queen came on the end, and that's a big deal! So he made a full house and knocked me down to almost nothing.

About four hands later when I was on the button, I picked up the A♣ 10♣ and got it all in against Erik Seidel, who had two fives. His fives held up like iron and I went out in fifth place. Once I went out, I thought that it would get down to Johnny Chan and Seidel, two great players, and indeed they came first-second. Ron Graham, who finished third, had a lot of chips but never wanted to play a flop—he always moved all his chips into the pot before it. Brenes and Graham are very good players, and Jim Bechtel, the man who came sixth, went on to win the big one in 1993. Quintin "Catbird" Nixon, who finished seventh, is a great player too. So, everybody at the final table was quite good.

WSOP CONCEPTS FROM 1990

17. A DRAMATIC AND INCREDIBLE HAND

1990 WSOP HEADS-UP
Hans "Tuna" Lund versus Mansour Matloubi
by Tom McEvoy

In 1990 Hans "Tuna" Lund faced off against
Mansour Matloubi for the championship,
the cash, and the bracelet. The blinds were
quite high, $15,000-$30,000. On the button
Lund went all in with pocket fours for about
$300,000. Matloubi called with pocket sixes,
so the pot was close to $700,000. Matloubi
had a substantial chip lead, so Lund definitely
was in trouble going into this hand. If Lund

had taken the pot, he would have been back in contention for the title, although he still would have been trailing in the chip count. The flop came 8-Q-2 with no help for either player on the turn and river. Mansour won the championship with a pair of sixes.

The highlight of the match-up between them was not the final hand, but one that occurred shortly before the showdown. On the button, Matloubi brought it in for a $75,000 raise with 10♦ 10♣. Lund, who was in the chip lead, called the raise with A♣ 9♦. The flop came 9♠ 2♣ 4♦, giving Lund top pair and top kicker, and Matloubi an overpair to the flop. Lund checked, Matloubi led off with a $100,000 bet, and Lund raised $250,000. Matloubi studied and thought, and finally called the $250,000 raise and reraised the rest of his chips, $378,000. Then it was Lund's turn to ponder. After a long pause, he shrugged his shoulders and called the raise. I think Lund knew that he was beaten at this point, but he had so much money already in the pot he just decided to go for it.

In one of the most dramatic hands in WSOP history, the A♠ hit on the turn, giving Lund the lead with two pair, aces and nines, against Matloubi's two tens. Matloubi had only two outs to win the pot, the two tens left in the deck, which was a 22 to 1 shot. There were 44 unseen cards—only two of them would give Matloubi the winning hand and 42 wouldn't help him at all. He was in a world of hurt.

When the ace hit on fourth street, Matloubi paced around the table nervously and actually kicked his chair. With all the money in, Lund had Matloubi covered and was set to become the world champion, unless a miraculous two-out 10 fell on the river—and that's exactly what happened! Matloubi caught the miracle 10♠, won the pot, which had over 80 percent of the chips in it, and went from runner-up to chip leader and eventual champion. Lund sat motionless and mute, crestfallen over the loss. Indeed it was a rags to riches hand for Matloubi.

The hand was so exciting to watch because the lead kept switching back and forth. It was one of the most dramatic flip-flopping World Series hands ever. In fact the announcer remarked, "This is the most incredible hand in WSOP history." This key hand changed the momentum of the tournament. Lund probably would not have gone broke with pocket fours on the final hand if he had not been forced to play a hand after his loss to Matloubi's tens— but the blinds were so high that he had to take a stand with something.

WSOP CONCEPTS FROM 1991

18. BIG SLICK VS. J-J VS. 8-8

1991 WSOP FIVE-HANDED
Brad Daugherty, Robert Veltri,
and Perry Green
by Tom McEvoy

In a key hand that turned the tide of the
tournament, Robert Veltri opened the betting
at $30,000. Brad Daugherty answered the bet
by going all-in with the A♣ K♦. Perry Green
responded from the blind by going all in with
the 8♥ 8♣. Veltri decided to overcall with the
J♣ J♥, creating a side pot between him and
Green. Daugherty was the short stack at this
point and if he lost the hand, would finish

fifth. If Veltri took it he would knock out two players. He was the favorite with two jacks, and he had a lot of chips at the time, but his overcall was marginal, to say the least.

The flop came A♦ Q♠ 7♠. The turn and river cards were the 3♠ 3♣. There were three spades on board, but since nobody had spades in his hand, Daugherty's aces won the pot. Veltri won the side pot against Green, sending the Alaskan out in fifth place. Green was interviewed after the hand and stated that he was very surprised when Veltri called the two all-in players with pocket jacks—it was just too risky against two all-in players. I tend to agree with him, although I still question Green playing the eights to start with, trying to shut out Veltri and get heads-up against Daugherty, whom he put on two big cards. Green read Daugherty correctly, but he didn't read Veltri right. He thought that he could move Veltri off his hand, but he got stubborn and called, won a substantial side pot, and broke Green.

The problem with Green's play was that Daugherty definitely had either two overcards or a pair bigger than the eights. And of course, Green didn't know what Veltri held—he must have raised with something, he was still to act, and he had more chips than Green. Green knew that Daugherty was very solid, and that against him alone he was either a slight favorite or a big underdog (if Brad had a higher pair). But with Veltri still to act, it was a marginal play. That pot had approximately a half million dollars in it, and with 215 players in the tournament there were $2,150,000 chips in play. After this hand, Brad had $500,000, putting him in third place.

19. THE IMPORTANCE OF THE BEST KICKER

1991 WSOP HEADS-UP
Brad Daugherty versus "Tucson" Don Holt

The final hand always ends the tournament, but the hand that gave Brad Daugherty half the chips and put him in a position to win came up before the last cards were dealt. Don Holt was the chip leader for most of the final table in 1991, but when it got down to heads-up play between Holt and Daugherty, they played a key hand that turned things around and switched the momentum in Daugherty's favor.

In this hand, Daugherty held an A-10 and Holt had a K-10. The flop came 4-5-10. Daugherty checked, Holt bet enough to put Daugherty all in, and Daugherty called. The turn card was a jack and the river card was a nine. There was a little over $1 million in this pot out of just over $2 million in play. Winning this hand gave Brad one-half of the chips in play, whereas if he had lost it, he would've been out of the tournament and Holt would have become the champion.

20. A GUTSHOT DRAW

1991 WSOP FINAL HAND
Brad Daugherty versus Don Holt
by Tom McEvoy

In the final hand of the tournament, Don Holt limped on the button with the 7♥ 3♥. Holding K♠ J♠, Daugherty raised $75,000. Holt made a minor mistake by limping on the button, although it only cost him half a bet and he had position. On the other hand, calling Daugherty's raise was Holt's big mistake.

The flop came 8♦ 9♥ J♣, giving Daugherty top pair and giving Holt a three-flush and a gutshot straight draw (a 10 would make a straight for him). Of course, if Daugherty had a queen in his hand, the 10 would give him an even higher straight. Daugherty checked the flop and Holt moved in for about $450,000. I think this was a bad play on Don's part because an 8-9-J flop can hit people in a lot of different ways, making it a dangerous flop to go up against. Nonetheless, here they were playing another million-dollar pot!

But this time Daugherty had the chip lead going in, and he didn't take much time to call Holt's semi-bluff. The 5♣ on the turn gave Holt eight outs to hit a straight (a 6 or a 10 would do it for him). But when the 8♠ came at the river, his drawing days were over and Daugherty became the 1991 world champion—and the first million-dollar winner at the World Series of Poker.

Holt had picked the wrong time to put all his chips in on an inside-straight draw. It is dangerous to bluff at coordinated flops because people will catch a part of it— especially when cards such as J-10 or J-9 come on the flop—and make a play at the pot. And that is exactly what happened in the final hand between Daugherty and Holt. Daugherty had trailed badly at one point and made a tremendous comeback to win the title.

WSOP CONCEPTS FROM 1992

21. WHEN A DRAW FALLS SHORT

1992 WSOP FOUR-HANDED
Hamid Dastmalchi-Mike Alsaadi-Tom Jacobs

A key hand came up when it was four-handed that put Tom Jacobs in a position to advance to heads-up play for the title against the eventual winner, Hamid Dastmalchi. With the blinds at $5,000-$10,000, Jacobs brought it in for $30,000 on the button. Both Alsaadi (small blind) and Dastmalchi (big blind) called, making it close to a $100,000 pot. The flop came K♦ 6♦ 4♣. Alsaadi, semi-bluffing, moved in on a flush draw with A♦ J♦, trying to win it right there. Dastmalchi thought about it and folded, and then it was Jacobs' turn to mull over his options. He had opened it pre-flop for $30,000 with the K♣ J♠ so he had flopped top pair with a mediocre kicker. He decided to play it and called Alsaadi's bet.

The turn was the Q♥ followed by the Q♠ on the river. If Jacobs had lost this pot, he would have been crippled and probably would have finished fourth. Instead he won it with a pair of kings and, because he had a few more chips, he sent Alsaadi to the rail in fourth place.

22. TOUGH DECISION- FOLDING POCKET KINGS

1992 WSOP-1999 7-HANDED

A very interesting hand came up on the third day of play at the 1992 Series when it was still seven-handed. (Only six players were filmed at the final table, a tradition that held until 2001, so seventh-place finisher Johnny Chan did not appear for the TV cameras.) The hand was contested by Mike Alsaadi and Hamid Dastmalchi, who was the chip leader. Dastmalchi raised before the flop with two kings and Alsaadi moved in on him. While

Dastmalchi thought about what he should do, Alsaadi announced that he had two aces.

If Dastmalchi called and lost, he would be in second place, although still in the tournament with a fairly good chip position. If he called and won, he would have an overwhelming chip lead. If he folded, he would retain his chip lead. Gently tapping the table, he turned over two kings and threw them in the muck. True to his word, Alsaadi flashes two aces.

Alsaadi didn't want to take the chance of getting drawn out on. I would've had a different perspective on how to play it, but Alsaadi was determined not to get his aces cracked so that he could make it to the final day — making good on his promise, made early in the tournament, to do exactly that.

But this wasn't the only time that a tournament leader holding two kings against two aces has made that kind of fold and then gone on to win the tournament. Seven years later at the 1999 Tournament of Champions in Las Vegas, a similar situation came up. David Chiu, the eventual winner, raised on the button with pocket kings when the action was still six or seven-handed. Louis Asmo, in the small blind and a distant second in chips, moved in with two aces. Chiu would have taken an overwhelming lead if he won the pot, although he still would have a pretty good chip lead if he folded. Chiu thought it over, tapped the table, and mucked the two kings. Asmo turned over his two aces for the audience to see. Eventually he came second to Chiu for the title. In these two scenarios, both Dastmalchi and Chiu protected their chip lead by folding pocket kings before the flop and went on to win the tournament.

23. BLUFFING, RAISING, RE-RAISING, FOLDING

1992 WSOP THREE-HANDED
Tom Jacobs versus Tuna Lund

This is a case where previous hands set the stage for Hans "Tuna" Lund's move. Lund had been bluffing and losing regularly—he raised, got reraised, and folded. After losing a whole series of pots, Lund probably was on tilt against the one player who was most likely to call him with a marginal hand. That's exactly what Tom Jacobs did.

With the blinds at $10,000-$20,000, Lund had about $175,000 left and moved all in with the 8♣ 7♠. Jacobs called with the K♦ 8♦, which isn't a very good hand, but when matched up against Lund's 8-7 offsuit it was a monster. The flop came 3♥ 5♦ 2♦.

On the turn Lund caught a 7 to make a pair. Unfortunately for him it was the 7♦, which gave Jacobs the winning flush. This hand put Lund out of the tournament and put Jacobs in a position to play Dastmalchi heads-up for the title.

If Lund hadn't lost a long string of hands prior to this one, the chances are good that he would not have gone slightly bonkers with his 8-7. In one prior hand Lund misplayed a big pocket pair against Dastmalchi—he didn't bet enough, a misplay that allowed Dastmalchi to hit a set of trips at the river to crack Lund's bigger pair, setting the stage for Lund's downfall. Chip Reese interviewed him after he went out, asking Lund whether he was "a little bit of a hot sucker." "No, not really," Lund answered, and then added that if Jacobs won the tournament, he would play him for the whole million later that night. Lund did admit, however, that he had made a mistake on the hand against Dastmalchi.

24. GOING HEADS-UP WITH A MARGINAL HAND

1992 WSOP FINAL HAND
Hamid Dastmalchi versus Tom Jacobs
by Tom McEvoy

The final hand of the 1992 WSOP interestingly demonstrates that sometimes you have to go all-in with some pretty marginal hands. Don't forget, though, that when you're playing heads-up the value of the hand changes because only two players are contesting each pot. It takes less strength to play, which means that you can play more marginal hands than you ordinarily would—and that's exactly what happened in this scenario.

In my opinion, Jacobs misplayed this final hand. Let me analyze it as to why I think so. With a little over $2 million in play, Dastmalchi had about a 2 to 1 chip lead. The blinds were $10,000-$20,000 with a $2,000 ante. Dastmalchi had 8♥ 4♣ and Jacobs held the J♦ 7♠, not very good starting hands. Jacobs called to see the flop for $10,000 on the button (which is the small blind in heads-up tournament play) and Dastmalchi checked.

The flop came J♥ 5♦ 7♦, giving Jacobs top-two pair and a three-flush. Dastmalchi didn't have any diamonds, but needed a 6 to make an inside straight.

This is where I think Jacobs made a mistake: On the flop, with $2 million chips in play and over $600,000 in his stack, Jacobs only bet $30,000 into a $44,000 pot. I think that he should have made a bigger bet, at least $50,000 or $60,000. With two diamonds and two connecting cards on board, there is a lot of drawing potential out there, especially in an unraised pot. Jacobs underbet, in my opinion, apparently trying to lure Dastmalchi into the pot.

Obviously, if Jacobs had raised before the flop, Dastmalchi probably would have folded. But on the flop, even though he was only drawing to an inside straight, $30,000 was only a minimal chip investment for Dastmalchi compared to the huge implied odds the pot offered him. He knew that if he hit his hand, he had a very good chance of busting Jacobs. And that's exactly what happened. By limping in before the flop and underbetting on the flop, Jacobs let him in too cheap.

The 6♥ peeled off on the turn and Dastmalchi checked his straight (which I think was the correct play). Jacobs moved his $600,000 all-in, overbetting the pot instead of underbetting it, with a connecting card on board. This was his second mistake; evidently he was trying to shut Dastmalchi out in case he was on a draw, which of course, he had already made. When the 8♣ fell at the river, Dastmalchi's hand held up, and his arms shot into the air as he became the 1992 WSOP champion.

WSOP CONCEPTS FROM 1993

25. KNOWING WHEN IT'S TIME TO SHUT DOWN

1993 WSOP THREE-HANDED
Jim Bechtel versus John Bonetti
by T.J. Cloutier

The table was down to three-way action between John Bonetti, Jim Bechtel, and Glen Cozen who was a distant third. I knew that Bechtel played every hand from behind, and I warned Bonetti about that. In the key hand Bonetti bet before the flop with A-K and Bechtel called him with pocket sixes. When the flop came K-6-4 Bonetti bet and Bechtel flat-called. Right then, neon lights should've started flashing in Bonetti's head. I understand that when you're in the heat of battle, sometimes you just don't see every opportunity, but you have to stay alert. Bonetti should've thought, "I've got all these chips and Glen Cozen only has a few. Am I gonna get broke in this pot, or am I gonna check it down and if Bechtel bets at me, throw this hand away?"

Essentially, Bonetti lost over $200,000 by making a hasty decision. I had told him earlier that Bechtel is weaker leading with a hand than he is calling with one. In other words, if Bechtel had been leading with his hand, Bonetti's A-K probably was good, but just calling, that was different. Once Bechtel called Bonetti, and taking into account his chip position versus Cozen, Bonetti had to shut down—he couldn't lose any more money to the hand because of the payouts.

But Bonetti didn't fold, and Bechtel won the hand with trip sixes, sending Bonetti out third and easing Cozen into second. The final hand between Bechtel and Cozen was anticlimactic, and Bechtel became the 1993 World Champion.

WSOP CONCEPTS FROM 1994

26. A STRAIGHT FLUSH DOUBLES UP THE WINNER

1994 WSOP SIX-HANDED
Russ Hamilton versus Vince Burgio

Going to the final six at the championship table, Vince Burgio was a solid second, well ahead of the players behind him, but trailing the leader, Hugh Vincent, who had almost three times as many chips. In this key hand, Burgio opened for $30,000 on the button and Russ Hamilton called with the K♣ J♣ from the blind. The flop came 6♣ 7♣ 10♣, giving Hamilton a king-high flush. He led at the pot for $15,000, which isn't a very big bet—it was a suck-in bet, actually. Burgio called.

The turn card was the 9♣ which put four cards to the straight flush on board. Hamilton appeared to be in jeopardy—he could be up against the ace-high flush or the nut straight flush. He checked, and Burgio did the same.

On the river the magic dream card hits for Hamilton—the Q♣. He had an unbeatable king-high straight flush, the only straight flush ever made at the championship table. Hamilton fired $80,000 at the pot and Burgio raised him another $80,000. Hamilton called all-in for approximately the size of the reraise and took the huge pot.

We can't know for sure what Burgio had because when Hamilton announced his straight flush, Burgio threw his cards in the muck. Hamilton doubled-up on this dramatic hand, putting him in contention and setting him up to eventually win the tournament.

27. THE DANGER OF CHECKING

1994 WSOP THREE-HANDED
Hugh Vincent versus John Spadavecchia

A pot was played three-handed at the 1994 championship table that was almost unbelievable. Holding the K♥ Q♣, John Spadavecchia opened the pot for a $50,000 raise. Hugh Vincent reraised Spadavecchia $100,000 with the 7♣ 6♣. Russ Hamilton folded and Spadavecchia called the raise. The flop came J♣ 7♦ 10♦, giving Spadavecchia an open-ended straight draw and two overcards, and Vincent a pair of sevens and a three-flush. Spadavecchia then did something that a lot of seasoned pros would not — he checked. Vincent answered with a bet of $250,000. With about $550,000 left in chips, Spadavecchia went all-in. Because of the size of the pot, he actually was forcing Vincent to gamble. Vincent called the raise.

As the first to act, if Spadavecchia had decided to make an all-in play on the flop, it's doubtful that Vincent could have called him with bottom pair. Calling the check-raise was marginal at best for Vincent, as was Spadavecchia's gamble. But since

Spadavecchia had shown some speed to his play, it may be that Vincent thought that he might not have as good a hand as he was representing.

The 2♣ came on the turn, giving Vincent a flush draw to go with his pair, followed by the harmless 3♠ on the river. Vincent won a huge pot, which put him close to Hamilton in the chip count and eliminated Spadavecchia, who finished in third place.

28. UNDERSTANDING WHEN AN OPPONENT IS POT-COMMITTED

1994 WSOP HEADS-UP
Russ Hamilton versus Hugh Vincent

When the play was heads-up between Hugh Vincent and Russ Hamilton, another incredible hand was unveiled. At this point Vincent had the lead with about $1.6 million and Hamilton had $1,070,000. Hamilton brought it in for $150,000 with Q♣ Q♠. Vincent called the raise with a 10-9 offsuit, a pretty marginal hand for that size of bet.

The flop came Q♥ 6♦ 5♥, giving Hamilton top set and giving Vincent nothing. Hamilton correctly checked the flop, trying to trap

Vincent into some sort of action; but Vincent didn't take the bait and checked behind him. Then the 8♠ appeared on fourth street. Vincent had a double-belly-buster straight draw—he could make a straight with either a jack or a seven. Hamilton fired $400,000 at the pot, leaving $500,000 in reserve. At this point he had a little more than one-half of his chips in the pot.

Now comes the part where Vincent misplayed his hand. Although Vincent had an out, it was apparent that Hamilton was pretty well pot-committed. All Vincent had on the turn was a 10 high hand with one card to come—and he decided to move in on Hamilton, a very questionable play. Since Hamilton had so many chips already in the pot, Vincent had to realize that there was a pretty good chance that he was going to call, which he did. The board paired on the end with the 8♣, giving Hamilton a full house, a giant pot, and the chip lead. Vincent's stack was reduced to around a half-million in chips. This $2 million pot was a WSOP record at that time.

WSOP CONCEPTS FROM 1995

29. THE IMPORTANCE OF THE CHIP COUNT

1995 WSOP FIVE-HANDED
Dan Harrington, Howard Goldfarb, Hamid
Dastmalchi, Brent Carter, and Barbara Enright

Five-handed at the final table of the 1995
WSOP, it seemed apparent that players were
making calls based on the chip counts of
their opponent rather than on the strength of
their hole cards. In the first scenario, Hamid
Dastmalchi was short-stacked against the
blinds. On the button he had J-10 suited and
moved in his last chips, worth $92,000. After
the small blind folded, Dan Harrington made

a very marginal call in the big blind with a J-3 offsuit. Even with a lot of chips, many pros would not have made that play. He was second in chips at that time, almost tied with Howard Goldfarb. Nothing came to help either of their hands, and Dastmalchi's J-10 won the pot, allowing him to double through Harrington with jack-high, no pair.

In the second scenario, Barbara Enright suffered a truly bad beat with by far the shortest stack, she was in the small blind with 8-8. Enright had just enough chips to make a decent raise. Holding the 6♦ 3♦ in the big blind, Brent Carter called.

Carter had a lot of chips and he gambled in a spot where a lot of other players would pass. The board came with the 6♥ 3♠ Q♥ 9♣ A♠, giving Carter two pair and sending the only female player ever to make it to the championship table to the rail. Enright was visibly disappointed at having to settle for fifth place. Her chip count contributed to her defeat just like Dastmalchi's let him doubling up against Hamilton.

In scenario three, the blinds were $15,000-$30,000 with three players left. Howard Goldfarb brought it in for a raise on the button, making it $90,000 to go with the A♥ 4♥. Brent Carter called with the K♠ Q♠. The flop came 8♥ 6♦ 5♥, giving Goldfarb the nut flush draw and an inside straight draw, plus the ace overcard. Carter decided to gamble with his K-Q suited and made a big move-in on Goldfarb. The pot grew to over $600,000. Goldfarb hardly even hesitated in calling Carter with what looked to be a drawing hand.

A more experienced player might have laid the hand down rather than put in that much money on a draw heads-up, but as it turned out, Goldfarb's A-4 was a monstrous favorite over Carter's K-Q since Carter had only four cards to pair up that wouldn't also make the flush for his opponent. Carter, of course, took a big risk in trying to take Goldfarb off his hand. The turn card was the 2♥ with a blank on the river, giving Goldfarb the nut flush and the pot, and racing Carter out of the tournament in third place.

30. THE EIGHTS WERE LOOKING GREAT

1995 WSOP FINAL HAND
Dan Harrington versus Howard Goldfarb

Dan Harrington had a pretty substantial chip lead when the final hand came down against Howard Goldfarb. On the button with

A♥ 7♣, Goldfarb was actually the pre-flop favorite over Harrington. With the blinds at $15,000-$30,000, he made a $100,000 bring-in bet. Harrington decided to gamble with the 9♦ 8♦ and called the raise. Goldfarb still had over $600,000 left, which was a substantial amount of chips.

The flop came 8♣ 6♦ 2♣, giving Harrington a pair of eights. He checked and Goldfarb moved his whole $600,000 into the pot. Without too much hesitation, Harrington called him with top pair and a mediocre kicker. There were a lot of hands that Goldfarb could have had that would beat Harrington, or he even could have had a strong draw, but basically, he was in there on a total bluff after the flop. The Q♠ and Q♥ came on the turn and river, helping neither player. Harrington won the hand and the championship with a pair of eights.

WSOP CONCEPTS FROM 1997

31. A DRAW VERSUS TWO PAIR

1997 WSOP SIX-HANDED
John Strzemp versus Mel Judah

A key hand came up between John Strzemp and Mel Judah when it was still six-handed at the 1997 championship table. The blinds were $5,000-$10,000 with an ante of $2,000. In first position, Judah raised $35,000 more holding the A♦ J♠. Strzemp decided to defend his big blind with the 9♣ 7♣, which was a marginal call, but he was gambling a little bit to get some chips. The flop came A♣ J♥ 8♣, giving Strzemp draws to a flush and an inside straight if a 10 came. Judah, of course, flopped top-two pair.

Strzemp decided to try to steal this pot and moved all-in with his remaining chips, and Judah called. The 3♣ came on the turn followed by the 10♦ at the river. This was a key pot because it enabled Strzemp to double up when he hit the flush on the turn card. When the 10♦ fell at the river, of course, Strzemp would have made the straight even if he had missed the flush. This hand left Judah shortstacked, although he managed to survive and come back to finish third, while Strzemp went on to finish second to Stu Ungar.

32. WHEN THE FLOP COMES A-K-X

1997 WSOP SIX-HANDED
Stu Ungar — Ron Stanley — John Strzemp

The final table was still six-handed when a three-way pot developed between Stu Ungar, Ron Stanley, and John Strzemp. Ungar was in the lead with a little more than $1 million in chips, Stanley was second with $850,000, and Strzemp was in third place. Stanley brought it in for a $45,000 raise, Ungar called on the button, and so did Strzemp in the big blind.

The flop came with an ace and a king, plus a small card. All three checked on the flop.

On fourth street, a blank came. Strzemp checked from the blind, Stanley bet $45,000, and Ungar called him. Strzemp folded. At the river, another raggedy-looking card came off. Stanley checked and Ungar value-bet $100,000. Stanley took his time thinking about it, as was his habit, and finally called the bet. Ungar turned over A-Q and scooped the pot.

The pot was around $300,000, so Ungar lifted a couple hundred thousand off Stanley's stack, which gave him about a 2 to 1 chip lead. Ungar's fairly passive play with A-Q in this key hand milked a $100,000 river bet out of Stanley, and set the stage for a later play in which he bluffed Stanley out of a key pot.

33. PLAYING A BIG BLUFF

1997 WSOP FOUR-HANDED
Stu Ungar versus Ron Stanley

A little while after Ungar had won that nice pot with his A-Q, another interesting hand came down, one that turned out to be key for Stanley. Ungar had inched a bit further out in front, but Stanley was still a solid second when a rather innocuous pot developed into something that really turned the tide against Stanley.

Stanley limped into the pot from the small blind for $5,000 with the 9♦ 7♦. Ungar had a Q-10 in the big blind and checked. The flop came A♠ 6♠ 9♥, giving nothing to Ungar and a pair of nines to Stanley, who decided to check the flop. Ungar also checked. If Stanley had made any kind of bet, it is probable that he would have won the pot right there.

The turn card was the 8♣. Stanley still had a pair of nines with an open-ended straight draw, and Ungar had picked up a gutshot straight draw if a jack hit on the river. Stanley decided to bet $25,000 at the pot, and Ungar raised him $60,000 more on a semi-bluff. If Stanley had an ace in his hand, Ungar couldn't win if he paired either the queen or the 10, but would have to hit the jack for the straight. Furthermore, if a 10 came it would give Stanley a straight so Ungar couldn't hit the 10 safely. He was hoping, of course, that Stanley would fold his hand.

Stanley thought and thought, and finally called the $60,000 raise. This set the stage for the river card, the K♦, which didn't help either player. But now there were two overcards on the board to Ron's pair of nines. He checked, and Ungar bet $220,000. Ron agonized at length before finally folding.

If Ungar hadn't made his big bet, he could not have won the hand in a showdown. After Stanley reluctantly folded, Ungar showed him the bluff by flashing his useless Q-10. Stanley was never the same after that. If he had made the call, he would have been fairly even with Ungar in the chip count and well ahead of the remaining players. Instead, his chip position eroded even further, but more importantly, so did his confidence.

34. THE LUCK FACTOR

1997 WSOP FINAL TABLE
John Strzemp versus Ron Stanley

A miracle hand unveiled itself at the '97 championship table that hastened Stanley's downfall and demonstrates how important luck can be in poker. Stanley brought it in for a raise with K♦ K♣, Ungar called, and Strzemp decided to move all-in for about $200,000 from the small blind with 10-10. Stanley reraised all in, and Ungar folded.

As is the custom when a player is all in, Stanley and Strzemp turned their cards face up. "I folded a 10," Mel Judah announced, meaning that only one 10 was left in the deck. The flop came 3♣ 6♣ 7♠. Amazingly, the turn card was the 10♦ — a 44 to 1 shot — followed by the 5♥ on the river. Stanley looked shocked, devastated; he had already lost a big pot to Ungar, been bluffed out of a pot by Ungar, and now he was beaten by Strzemp's one-out hand. This loss dropped Stanley from second to third in the chip count and he went straight downhill from there.

Remember how we talked about how the play of a previous hand often sets the stage for a subsequent hand that either busts you out of the tournament or makes your day? Here is the final, fatal hand for Ron Stanley. John Strzemp played it very cagey in the blind with A-A. Stanley made it $60,000 to go with a J-8 offsuit, a stone cold bluff on his part. Strzemp flat-called the raise.

The flop came something like K-7-2 rainbow and Strzemp led at the pot. Apparently deciding that Strzemp was on a bluff, Stanley moved all-in on him—with no pair, no draw, and no hope. Strzemp called and won the pot, moving Stanley out of the tournament in fourth place. But if Stanley hadn't lost the previous series of other hands, it is highly unlikely that he would have done what he did—which was commit poker suicide, basically.

35. WHEN THE FLOP SHOULD BE BET

1997 WSOP THREE-HANDED
Stu Ungar versus Mel Judah

With three players left, Mel Judah opened on the button for $60,000 with the 10♥ 9♣, which is not a very strong hand. Ungar called the raise from the small blind with the Q♦ J♣, and Strzemp folded in the big blind.

The flop came J♥ 3♥ 10♦ — Ungar had top pair with a reasonable kicker and Judah had the second-best pair. Ungar checked the flop and so did Judah. The 2♣ came on the turn, which didn't help either player. This time Ungar led $80,000 at the pot. Judah called the bet and raised another $162,000. Ungar called, making a huge pot of over $600,000. The K♣ hit on the river and Ungar's pair of jacks won the pot.

Looking back, Judah probably should have bet something on the flop just to define his hand. When Ungar bet on fourth street, he absolutely convinced Judah that he was either on a draw or was bluffing — Judah just wouldn't have made a $162,000 raise with second pair otherwise. He still had five outs, of course, but he was in terrible shape. Ungar thought before calling the raise—he had entered the pot with a marginal hand to start with, but he had a lot of chips and wasn't taking a big risk, so the call was correct.

Ungar just played beautifully and trapped Judah. At least if Judah had bet the flop and Ungar had moved in Judah probably could've gotten away from his hand. And if Ungar had flat-called a bet on the flop, Judah could've shut down the rest of the way and not gone broke.

Ungar went on to win his third championship against runner-up John Strzemp when he outdrew Strzemp's A-8 with by catching a deuce at the river to make a wheel with his A-4. It was not the first time that Ungar had won the championship with a wheel: In 1980 he outdrew Doyle Brunson's A♥ 7♥ when he played a 5♠ 4♠. The flop came A-7-2, giving Brunson top-two pair and Ungar an inside-straight draw. Ungar caught a 3 on fourth street to complete the wheel.

Although Ungar and Johnny Moss both are credited with being three-time World Champions of Poker, Ungar is the only player in history to have won the title against three full fields of opponents. Moss was voted the champion in 1970 (the only year when the champion was decided by a vote, instead of playing down to the last man standing as was done in the other championships) and defeated a total of 20 opponents to win the title in 1971 and 1974. Ungar, by contrast, defeated 72 players in 1980, 74 in 1981, and 311 in 1997.

WSOP CONCEPTS FROM 1998

36. POCKET ROCKETS HIT THE DUST

1998 WSOP SEVEN-HANDED
Scotty Nguyen versus Ben Roberts
by T.J. Cloutier

The 1998 final table wasn't nearly as exciting as the one that I played in 1988, but it was still a very good one. We started the televised action with only five players instead of the usual six because of an odd situation that came up when we were seven-handed.

I felt that the man who deserved to be at the televised table with us was Ben Roberts, because he is such a fine player, but he went out earlier, on this play: Jan Lundberg moved all in with two tens and Scotty called on the button with the A♦ Q♦. Ben moved in from the small blind for all his chips with pocket aces, and Scotty quickly called.

Everybody in the world knew that Ben had two aces, but Scotty called him fast with his suited ace. If Scotty had lost the hand, his stack would have been severely depleted and Ben would have had a substantial stack to make a run at the roses. The flop came with three diamonds and Scotty knocked Roberts and Lundberg out at the same time. That's why we only started with five players at the televised table, the only time that has ever happened in World Series history.

37. THE IMPORTANCE OF READING A BIGGER HAND

1998 WSOP THREE-HANDED
T.J. Cloutier versus Kevin McBride
by T.J. Cloutier

When the action got down to Scotty Nguyen, Kevin McBride, and me at the final table, I folded pocket jacks twice, which is hard to do three-handed. Both times Kevin had pocket kings, and both times he played them the same way, going slow in the middle and calling a raise. The first time, Scotty brought it in for $40,000, Kevin called, and I reraised it. Scotty threw his hand away and Kevin called my raise. The flop came raggedy, I bet, and Kevin came over the top of me. I threw my jacks away and he showed me two kings.

About a half an hour later, Scotty brought it in for a raise, Kevin called, and again I had two jacks. This time I made a smaller raise, and Scotty and Kevin both called. The board came 8 high. "Boy, I wonder if I'm in the same situation again?" I thought. So, I made a little bet at the pot—I wasn't about to make a big bet like I did the time before. Scotty threw his hand away and Kevin came over the top again. I said "Adios, amigos!" and mucked the jacks. Kevin showed me two kings again. Those were two tough laydowns.

On the final hand that I played, Kevin raised from the little blind and I reraised him with K-Q in the big blind, knowing that I had the best hand. He called my all-in raise with J♠ 9♠. The flop came with two spades, giving him a flush draw. But instead of another spade, he caught a jack and I was gone in third place in my third final-table appearance.

38. RAISE OR JUST MAKE A CRYING CALL?

1998 WSOP HEADS-UP
Scotty Nguyen versus Kevin McBride
by T.J. Cloutier

In heads-up play, a key hand came up between Kevin McBride and Scotty Nguyen in which there was an ace, a queen, and a 10 on the board at the end. Although there might've been a small raise before the flop, neither player bet until the river. Kevin made aces and queens, and Scotty made a straight with K-J, the nuts. Kevin bet it, Scotty raised, and Kevin called.

The only hand that Scotty could raise with in this pot would certainly beat top two pair, because he knew that he didn't have to take a shot in this spot. He had the lead in chips and didn't need to bluff Kevin. Kevin could've made a crying call at the end, but never should have called a raise. This pot was key because it left Kevin short on chips in heads-up play.

39. THE FATEFUL A-Q

1998 WSOP KEY HAND
Scotty Nguyen versus The Field
by T.J. Cloutier

Ace-queen was a big hand for Scotty Nguyen all through the tournament. In the hand that I just discussed, Nguyen made a straight with K-J to defeat McBride's A-Q. Earlier Scotty held A-Q against Jack Keller's pocket queens, caught an ace and won that hand. So, A-Q worked for Scotty repeatedly — and I couldn't win with the damn thing!

Here's how the pot with Keller came down: Before the final table began, Nguyen raised with the A♦ Q♦ and Keller moved all in with pocket queens for about $70,000 in chips. Nguyen almost beat him into the pot, before catching an ace and winning. Most players would have laid down A-Q against Keller's raise, but not Nguyen.

Later Scotty knocked out Ben Roberts and Jan Lundberg in the same hand just before we went to the final six. Then he played an A-Q heads up against McBride and made a straight to beat him. He played A-Q four times, won with it four times, and wound up winning the world championship. Of course Scotty got very lucky with A-Q, and that's important in tournament play. So often, it's *when* you make these types of plays that counts—timing is everything.

A-Q was Scotty's ticket to the top in 1998, but it was a terror for me in 2000 when I played it for the bracelet and the big bucks against Chris Ferguson's A-9.

WSOP CONCEPTS FROM 2000

40. 11 TO 10 FAVORITE OR 4.5 TO 1 DOG

2000 WSOP 7-HANDED
Chris Ferguson versus Jeff Shulman
by T.J. Cloutier

Before the final televised table, Chris Ferguson won a hand that put him in a position to really do damage later in the round (when he had aces against kings). Here's how it happened: Everyone folded to Jeff Shulman on the button and he brought it in for a raise with pocket sevens. The small blind folded, and Ferguson then came over the top from the big blind for all his chips with pocket sixes.

Shulman called the raise.

Shulman had $1,500,000 in chips and did not have to play any huge pots. He was playing super, but he was still inexperienced at that time. In that situation, you have to figure that you are an 11 to 1 favorite or a 4.5 to 1 dog. You don't figure that you're a 4.5 to 1 favorite when you're holding two sevens in that spot because Ferguson had reraised. If Ferguson had two overcards, even if they were only 9-8, Shulman was only an 11 to 10 favorite.

I don't think that Shulman was wrong in raising the pot a little bit (he had plenty of chips), but when Ferguson reraised, I believe that Shulman should have released the hand. He didn't need to gamble, and losing nothing more than the raise he put in wouldn't hurt too much. As it turned out, Ferguson made trip sixes and doubled through Shulman, putting himself in position to win the whole ballgame.

41. ONLY HAND IT COULD BE: ACES

2000 WSOP 7-HANDED
Ferguson versus Shulman, Again
by T.J. Cloutier

The next key hand happened after Ferguson won with pocket sixes against Shulman's sevens. He brought it in for a little raise under the gun and I reraised with pocket jacks, making it $200,000 to go. Shulman moved in for all his chips with pocket kings and Ferguson called. Obviously, I knew that my hand was a loser and I wasn't even going to call Shulman's reraise, so I released my hand, leaving me with $200,000, which I took to the final day.

When Shulman reraised and Ferguson called, there was only one hand in the world that Ferguson could've held—pocket aces. His aces beat Shulman's kings and in the process, sent Shulman to the rail in seventh place, setting up the final table. Although Shulman had the lead before these two key hands happened, double the chips of anybody else, these two hands took him out of action. That's all it takes to lose a tournament.

42. CHIPPING AWAY STRATEGY

2000 WSOP HEADS-UP
Ferguson versus Cloutier
by T.J. Cloutier

When we started the final table, Chris Ferguson had a lot of chips, the four others were close with $400,000 or more, and I had $216,000. When I got up that morning, I formed a plan that I explained to my wife: "I'll let them knock each other out and try to get heads up with Chris."

Since I believe that poker is a game of mistakes, I wanted to let the others make the errors, putting me in a position where I had a chance to win. They were all fine players, but none of them were experienced in final table play except Chris. That's why I thought that they would make major mistakes in crucial spots—and as it came up, that's exactly what happened. They dropped like flies.

The biggest element in this whole championship was that when we started playing heads up, Chris had $4,700,000 in chips and I had $400,000—and I took the lead away from him. Never at any time did I get my money in with the worst hand. I kept chipping away at him, which means that I was trying to get Chris to take me off in spots — and he did.

If I flopped a set and checked it to him, Chris would always catch some card that he thought was good enough to call with. When I had the best hand, I tried to let him pay, but not enough that it would make him drop his hand because I wanted to get paid on all those hands — that's what chipping away means. In other words, I tried to make bets that I figured he would call. And he was getting nervous about it — I could see it in his eyes and mannerisms. His hands were shaking so badly that he pulled them behind his mountain of chips to conceal his tremors.

I could see that he was getting worried, and I thought there might be a chance that he was going to make a major error on a hand — and he did when he called my all-in bet with A-9 when I held A-Q. But luck is a part of poker, and he caught a 9 on the river that won the title for him.

The way Chris explained it made sense to me — he said he thought that on that one day, he couldn't beat me if we just played out the hands. He thought that he had to beat me in a major pot, so he just decided to go with the hand. Obviously Chris thought that if he caught an ace, he'd have a hand but he was in horrible position. The interesting part is that it was his 9 kicker that made his hand a winner, not the ace. And you know what? I saw that 9 coming before the dealer ever peeled it off. It was as though I was looking right through the deck. It had happened twice before when he drew out to tie me when the board paired on the end.

WSOP CONCEPTS
FROM 2001

43. SLOW-PLAYING KINGS

2001 WSOP
Phil Hellmuth versus Layne Flack
by T.J. Cloutier

"It was a matchup made in poker heaven," the tournament reporter wrote. "Phil Hellmuth, the 1989 WSOP champ with six bracelets in 25 finishes versus T.J. Cloutier, the all-time (tournament) money winner with 33 finishes. Layne Flack, who finished third, also brought two bracelets to the table and Steve Rydel added one more."

When Hellmuth and I got heads-up for the title—which he eventually won—he had nearly a 3 to 1 edge over me in chips. When somebody asked me for a chip count, I replied, "Slightly lopsided." But as often happens, the key hand at the final table was not played heads-up between the two finalists—it happened earlier when Hellmuth beat Layne Flack in an unraised pot when it was down to three players. At the time, we were all about even in chips. I was not in the hand; Hellmuth and Flack played it heads up.

After the original bring-in and call, the flop came Q-2-6 rainbow. Both players checked, and fourth street brought a 9. Hellmuth made a bet of about $25,000 and Flack raised $50,000 more. Thinking that Flack was bluffing, Hellmuth called the raise holding A-6. Fifth street brought another 6, and when Flack moved all in Hellmuth finally realized that Flack must have had a hand when he bet on fourth street. However, unless Flack had filled at the river, Hellmuth knew that he had the best hand with trip sixes and an ace kicker. Catching that third six was the key moment at the final table—Hellmuth called Flack's all-in bet and won the pot, sending Flack out in third place. Later Flack confided to me that he had slow-played pocket kings.

The play of this hand goes to prove that no matter how well, or in some circumstances how badly, you play a hand, Lady Luck has a big say in no-limit hold'em.

44. A GAME OF MISTAKES

2001 WSOP FIVE-HANDED
Phil Hellmuth versus Carlos Mortenson
by T.J. Cloutier

Five-handed at the final table, the blinds were $15,000-$30,000 with a $6,000 ante, costing each player $75,000 a round to sit out. In a hand that combined what Andy Glazer referred to as "comedy, drama, triumph, and disaster," Phil Hellmuth limped into the pot, as did Phil Gordon on the button, Carlos Mortensen from the small blind, and Stan Schrier from the big blind, making it a four-way pot. The flop came 4♠ Q♠ 9♦. Both blinds checked, Hellmuth bet $60,000, Gordon folded, and Mortensen raised $200,000. After about a two-minute pause, Schrier (who hadn't realized it was his turn to act) also folded. It took Hellmuth only about 10 seconds to announce, "I'm all in!" as he pushed his remaining chips to the center of the table. Mortensen called.

When the hands were turned up, Hellmuth showed Q-10 to Mortensen's Q-J. A jack came on fourth street, giving Mortensen two pair and Hellmuth an open-ended straight draw. Hellmuth needed either an 8 or a king to make the straight. When the A♠ fell at the end, Hellmuth's $1 million in chips fell into Mortensen's stack and the 1989 World Champion of Poker darted out the door in fifth place.

This hand is a prime example of how even a great player like Phil Hellmuth can suffer a complete mental block on a hand. As I have written many times in our books, no-limit hold'em is a game of mistakes, and you want to be the player who makes the fewest. Unless you have an extremely big hand after the flop, when you are playing in an unraised pot you should never—and I stress *never*—give yourself a chance to lose all your chips when you have a decent amount of them to start with.

I see nothing wrong with Phil's original bet of $60,000. He had top pair and was trying to win the pot right there without giving any free cards. But when Carlos raised $200,000, Phil made mistake number one by calling the raise, because all he could beat was a bluff. Not only did he call the raise, Phil moved all-in against a very good and very aggressive player—mistake number two. Remember that this was an unraised pot. Why would anyone risk losing all his money in this situation?

When you analyze this play, you will conclude that there are very few hands that Mortensen could have raised with unless he was on a stone bluff. These hands include two overcards and a flush draw, but as this was an unraised pot, that's not likely. Ace-little-card of spades is one drawing hand that an aggressive player like Mortensen might raise with, but in this spot, I think that the J♠10♠ would be the most likely, in which case he would be favored over one pair.

All the other hands (two pair, a small set, K-Q, or Q-J) are big favorites over Hellmuth's Q-10. If Hellmuth had thought it through before acting, he would not have made mistake number one, let alone mistake number two. All it takes is one major error to reduce all of your good play in a tournament to naught.

WSOP CONCEPTS FROM 2002

45. A NIGHTMARE OF ACES

2002 FOUR QUEENS CLASSIC
David Ulliott Versus Lady Luck
by T.J. Cloutier

Sometimes you can play great poker throughout an event and still have absolutely no chance to win—David Ulliott is living testimony to that. He was the victim of Lady Luck in a series of events that you couldn't dream in your worst nightmare. In just one round of cards at the championship table, Ulliott held aces twice and kings once—and when all was said and done, he was broke!

Losing with his kings when his opponent

flopped an ace was bad enough, but it was only a precursor to what was to come. Next he raised the pot with pocket aces, only to see everyone fold so that the only payday he won was the antes.

The second time he picked up aces, he got all his chips in before the flop against James Ferrel, who held pocket queens. Ulliott's dream of winning the championship faded away when the flop came Q-6-4 with no help on fourth or fifth street for his aces, sending him out in eighth place.

I also was at this final table, which was dramatic in that an unusual number of big pairs seemed to be dealt. For example Jerri Thomas picked up pocket queens. She raised and Bruce Corman, who had pocket aces, reraised. She called the raise all in, but unfortunately, no ladies came on the flop this time and Jerri went out in seventh place.

Meanwhile, with all the big hands that were being dealt, I just sat there dead with no playable cards waiting for something that I could play—and making money by moving up another notch on the pay-scale every time somebody went out. Starting near the bottom of the heap, I managed to finish in third place behind Bruce Corman and Chris Karagulleyan. Sometimes patience is a profitable virtue.

TOURNAMENT TALK WITH T.J. AT THE FINAL TABLE

by Tom McEvoy

In one of the most dramatic finishes in the history of the World Series of Poker, Chris Ferguson was crowned the millennium's first World Champion of Poker, but T.J. Cloutier came within a heartbeat of finally capturing the coveted title that he has come so close to winning three times in the past, coming up short by one river card. It was T.J.'s second runner-up finish; he also has finished third and fifth. It was a heartbreaker for T.J., who had clawed back from a 10 to 1 chip deficit heads-up and at one point had taken the lead over Chris.

After T.J. made a fantastic comeback from such a big chip deficit to actually pull ahead, the action seesawed back and forth. The last pot was played all-in before the flop, with around $4.6 million of the $5.1 million chips in play, the largest single pot in WSOP history. The only thing that I've ever seen similar to that happened in 1982 when Dewey Tomko played Jack Straus heads-up for the championship. Dewey had the lead on the flop only to have it snatched from him at the river. With all the money in the middle, that hand settled the tournament. Similarly, with such a huge amount of money at stake and considering his other near misses, it truly was torture for T.J. as his A-Q fell to Chris's A-9 when a 9 came at the river to give Chris the win.

Coming to the final table with the shortest stack, T.J.'s vast tournament experience helped him wade through the other four players at the final table. He successfully avoided most major confrontations, and when he did play a hand he usually didn't get called. The one time that he was called, T.J. doubled through his adversary. He did the bob-and-weave until he got heads-up with Ferguson, when he opened up his game. Then he played a very controlled, aggressive style, coming over the top with several reraises, causing Chris to lay down multiple hands. It was an excellent example of cat-and-mouse poker, with T.J.'s short stack the cat and Chris's larger stack of chips the mouse.

Looking at the long haired, bearded Chris wearing sunglasses and a black felt hat with its brim curled low, I could almost feel his intensity. He looked determined, almost fierce, and the audience could see how badly he wanted to win. It's just unfortunate that one of them had to lose.

After coming back from such a big deficit, losing at the end was all the more disappointing for T.J. When the fatal river card fell, T.J. took it like the man that he is, not even flinching. At the exact moment that the killer 9 hit the felt, I looked at T.J.'s face—he didn't show much emotion, which is one reason why he's always been considered one of the best tournament players that ever lived, but I knew that he was in pain. After such a truly bad beat, T.J. shook hands with Chris, congratulated him, and then began the inevitable interviews from the multitude of media covering the event.

The grand finale of the WSOP was a celebration for Chris—who earlier had won the $5,000 seven-card stud title, making him the only double-bracelet winner in the 2000 WSOP—while at the same time I could feel T.J.'s heartbreak. A total gentleman, Chris told me with complete sincerity, "I feel terrible for T.J.," because he knew how brutal losing like that could be.

Without a doubt, T.J. is the greatest player never to have won the "Big One." But as they said in Brooklyn all those years before the Dodgers moved to Los Angeles, "Wait till next year." And actually, "next year" finally came once for the Brooklyn Dodgers—they won their own World Series in 1955 by beating the dreaded New York Yankees.

The day after the Series ended, I drove T.J. to McCarran Airport to catch a plane to Dallas—he was going home at last (about $900,000 richer, I might add). Along the way, I became so engrossed in our conversation about the play at the final table that T.J. had to give me several tips—not about poker but how to get to the airport!

How are you feeling after your near miss in the championship event? I asked.

"I'm feeling fine—how can you squawk at winning $896,000?! I thought that I played well, in fact as good as I've ever played in my life. After coming back from almost nothing, I got my chips in there three different times and each time I had Chris in situations where he had to outdraw me. You can't do any better than that. The first time, he had to pair the board to tie me; the second time, he had to match my high card on the board to tie; and the third time he had to catch a 9 down the river with three outs for all the money. When we started playing heads-up he had $4,700,00 and I had $400,000. I chopped my way back to where I was equal with him, so I can't fault my play. Lady Luck came into the picture this time, that's all."

You certainly gave a classic performance on how to play a short stack.

"Every time I got my money in, I got it in with the best hand. (Get on the freeway here, Tom.)"

You did indeed and that's all that anybody can do. It was cruel to lose to a three-outer like that.

"You just have to get a little lucky. (Now get in the left lane, okay?) All you can do is play your best and hope for a few breaks here and there. Of course, I had a game plan going into the final table. My plan was to let Chris destroy the other ones, or let them destroy themselves, and then try to take him off. I wanted to get to at least second place, but I knew that I was short-chipped and so for the time being, I stayed out of Chris's road. I worked on Hassan in one hand and that was all. Chris broke all the rest of them, and that was perfect. Every now and then, a game plan works."

Your tournament experience helped you wade through the other four finalists. It seems to me that the player with the biggest disappointment at the Series might have been newcomer Jeff Shulman, who went from the chip lead seven-handed to out of the tournament in about 20 minutes' time.

"I was playing at Shulman's table. He was very aggressive, but he also became just a little bit 'chip happy,' I think. Ferguson moved all his chips in with a pair of sixes and Shulman called him with a pair of sevens. He had the best hand, don't misunderstand me, but with his chip lead he didn't need to make this play—he didn't need to be involved in the pot at all. At the time, the handwriting was on the wall: Shulman had $1.5 million and doubled Ferguson up when a 6 flopped. Ferguson got lucky, sure, but there was no reason in the world for Shulman to have played a big pot in that spot with two sevens. (Turn right here, Tom.)"

Surely this was a key moment seven-handed and a more experienced player probably would have passed it. The other key hand happened when you, Chris, and Jeff were involved in a three-way pot later in the action.

"Yes. In the last pot of the night, the blinds were $15,000-$30,000 and Chris brought it in for $90,000. I raised it to $390,000 with pocket jacks—I didn't want anybody with a lone ace calling me. Jeff, who was sitting behind me with pocket kings, moved all-in. Then Chris also moved all-in. I knew that my two jacks were toilet paper, so I threw them away. One of them was going to get broke on the hand and I was going to get to the final table. Chris had pocket aces and they stood up against Jeff's pocket kings."

A pair of kings is hard to get away from. Of course, Chris wouldn't have been in the position to break him if Jeff hadn't already been in that previous hand with two sevens. Had he made any other plays that you questioned?

"No, he played aggressively, raising with a lot of ace-type hands like A-10 or A-6 from around back all the time. At an earlier table, I had played back at Jeff a couple of times. One time he thought that I might be on a stone bluff and took about five minutes to think it through. He was considering coming back over the top of me with his A-K, but instead he mucked the hand. I had two kings in the hole, which I showed to him. 'Boy, I had a real bad read on you there,' he said. (Go straight here, okay, Tom?)"

Looks like he did the right thing "by accident." But getting back to the final table action, there was no doubt in anyone's mind that if you had won that last hand, Chris would have been in a lot of trouble. At the end, Chris mentioned how well you played.

"Chris was very gracious to me. I thought that overall I played well in the tournament and so did he. Heads-up with me, Chris kept putting himself in situations where he had to call big bets with weak hands. I wasn't willing to put myself in that type of situation."

I thought that Chris might've been a little bit intimidated by you, and he suddenly quit catching cards for a while.

"He caught A-K or aces twice, but both

times I threw my hand away so that he didn't get any play on them. One time I had A♦ Q♦ and flat called. Things like that kept him from knowing exactly where I was coming from, which was my whole idea with those plays. In that particular hand, the flop came 6-4-2 with two diamonds. He bet about $60,000 and I just called with two overcards and the nut flush draw. A queen came at the river and I bet. He called, I showed him the queen and won the pot. I had read the hand correctly."

You took the lead and then it seesawed back and forth a bit.

"Yes, I had a small lead and then he won a pot. At the end I had $2.3 million to his $2.8 million. If I had won the last hand, he would've had only $500,000 left. (Departing flights are to the left.)"

As I understand it, no deal was made.

"That's right. I don't see how any kind of deal could have been discussed since Chris had such a big lead on everybody. Before we started playing, though, Roman Abinsay came to me and asked if I wanted to make a five-way deal with him and the other three players. 'I don't want to make any deal,' I said. 'I want to win it.'"

Chris certainly gave a good account of himself at the final table. What about your other four opponents?

"They all played well. I don't think, though, that they knew how to play their stacks in order to move up in the money. They could've made better choices of which hands to play when we were five and six-handed."

I agree, but with you coming from so far back to take second, this was one of the most dramatic World Series final tables that I've ever seen. The 9 that hit Chris this year on the end was a $600,000 river card plus the world championship. But I was surprised that he called your all-in raise with only an A-9.

"Chris himself said that he thought that I was outplaying him at that point and that his only chance of beating me was to gamble and hope to get lucky. I don't fault him on that. If it had been meant to be, I would have won it. But I'll stack my record up against all of them—four final-table finishes with a second and a third in the last three years."

You and Doyle Brunson are the only players who have placed in the top five four times. Stu Ungar won three times and was ninth one other time. Brunson had two firsts, a second and a third.

"And I plan to make it again next year or however long it takes."

We're almost at the airport terminal, T.J., so I just want you to know that I think you handled defeat like a gentleman.

"How could I have handled it any differently? I felt that if I went down, it would be on the last card. Maybe next time that river card will belong to me. (How did we get to Terminal Two, Tom? We want Terminal One, don't we?)"

Ooops!

TOURNAMENT POKER TERMS

Add On - A stack of chips that players have the option to purchase at the end of the tournament's re-buy period (the last opportunity you have to buy chips in a re-buy event.) "I *added on* at the end of the re-buy period to beef up my stack."

Any Ace - An ace with a weak kicker. "Some people will play *any* ace from late position in a tournament."

Backdoor a Flush/Straight - Make a hand that you were not originally drawing to by catching favorable cards on later streets. "I was betting top pair, but when a fourth spade hit at the river, I *backdoored* a flush."

Backer - Someone who pays the entry fees for a tournament player, and then splits the reward with the player at the end of the event.

Backup - A card that provides you with an extra out. "If you have a drawing hand, you like to have a *backup* to your draw, a secondary draw that might make your hand the winner."

Beat into the Pot - When an opponent bets an inferior hand, you gladly push your chips into the pot. "When three clubs came on the flop, Slim moved in. I *beat him into the pot* with my flush—he had a 10-high flush, mine was higher."

Behind (Sitting) - You have the advantage of acting after someone else acts. "So long as you're sitting *behind* the other players, you have the advantage of position."

Buy-In - The amount of money it costs to enter a tournament. The cost of the buy-in is often used to describe the size of a tournament. "He didn't have enough money for the *buy-in* to the $1,000 hold'em event, so he sold pieces of his action to three other players."

Big Ace - An ace with a big kicker (A-K or A-Q). "When the flop came A-6-2, I played my *big ace* strong."

Big Flop - The flop comes with cards that greatly enhance the strength of your hand. "I caught a *big flop* that gave me the nut flush."

Boss Hand - The best possible hand. "When you have the *boss hand*, you should bet it as aggressively as possible, especially if you think your opponents have drawing hands."

Broken Board - The board cards are random with no pair, flush, or straight possibilities. "A *broken board* such as 9-5-2 is a fabulous flop to pocket jacks."

Bully - To play aggressively. "When I have a big stack in a tournament, I like being able to *bully* the entire table."

Case Chips - Your last chips. "He raised all in with his *case chips*."

Change Gears - To adjust your style of play from fast to slow, from loose to tight, from raising to calling, and so on. "When the cards quit coming his way, Will didn't *change gears*; instead, he kept on playing fast and lost his whole bankroll."

Chip Status - How the number of chips that you have in front of you compares to those of your opponents.

Cold Call - To call a raise without having put an initial bet into the pot. "Bonetti raised, Hellmuth reraised, and I *cold called*."

Come Over the Top - Raise or reraise. "I raised it $2,000 and Sexton *came over the top* of me with $7,000."

Commit Fully - Put in as many chips as necessary to play your hand to the river, even if they are your case chips. "If I think the odds are in my favor, I will *commit fully*."

Confrontation - A big pot that usually is contested heads up and often significantly changes the players' chip status or alters the outcome of the tournament.

Cutoff Seat - The seat immediately in front of the button. "He raised from the *cutoff seat* to try to shut out the button and the blinds."

Decision Hand - A hand that requires you to make a value judgment. "The great hands and the trash hands play themselves. It is the *decision hands* that will determine your profit at the end of the session, the day, the year. It is all of the marginal, in-between hands that are played well that separate winners from losers. A-K is one of the biggest decision hands in poker."

Flat Call - Calling a bet without raising. "When he bet in to me, I just *flat called* to keep the players behind me from folding."

Flop to It - The flop enhances the value of your hand. "If you don't *flop to it*, you can get away from the hand."

Freeze-Out Tournament - When your original buy-in is gone, you cannot re-buy or add on extra chips to remain in play. "All WSOP events are *freeze-out* tournaments."

Get into the Deck - Get a free card. "If you just check your one-pair hand, you allow your opponents to *get into the deck*."

Get Away From It - To fold, usually when what appeared to be a premium hand catches an unfavorable flop that negated its potential. "If you don't flop to your hand, *get away from it*."

Get the Right Price - The pot odds are favorable enough for you to call a bet or a raise with a drawing hand. "Since I was getting the *right price*, I called the bet with a wraparound."

Get Full Value - To bet, raise, and reraise to manipulate the size of the pot so that you will win the maximum number of chips if you win the hand. "By raising on every round, I was able to get *full value* when my hand held up at the river."

Get There - You make your hand. "When you *get there*, you might be able to start maximizing your bets."

Give Them - You attribute a hand to your opponents. "When the flop comes with a pair and your opponent raises, what are you going to *give him*? A straight draw?!"

Isolate - You raise or reraise to limit the action to yourself and a single opponent. "I raised on the button to *isolate* against the big blind."

Increment - The increase in chips required to post the blinds and antes at the start of a new round in a tournament. When the blinds rise from $25-$50 to $50-$100, the increment has doubled.

Jammed Pot - The pot has been raised the maximum number of times and may also be multiway. "You should pass with a weak hand if the pot has been *jammed* before it gets to you."

Key Card - The one card that will make your hand a winner. "I knew that I needed to catch a 10, the *key card* to my straight draw."

Key Hand - A hand that turns the tide of fortune in a tournament. "The key hand that put me in a position to win came when I hit the flush at the river and won a huge pot."

Lay it Down - Fold. "Many times, you can put enough pressure on the pot to blow everybody away and sometimes even get the raiser to *lay down* his hand."

Limp - Enter the pot by just calling. "I decided to just *limp* in with a pair of tens and see the flop as cheap as possible."

Limper - A player who enters the pot for the minimum bet. "When there are two *limpers* already in the pot, a pair of jacks should be your minimum raising hand."

(Two) Limper Rule - Once two or more people have voluntarily entered the pot for the minimum bet, the hand has already shaped up to be multiway. "Small pairs and connectors become somewhat more attractive in middle to late position when *two or more players have limped* into the pot in front of you."

Live Cards - Cards that you need to improve your hand and which probably are still available. "When three players who I knew to be big-pair players entered the pot in front of me, I thought that my middle connectors might still be *live* so I decided to play the hand."

Long Call - To take a long time to decide whether to call a bet with a marginal hand. "When making a *long call*, your opponents can get a read on you."

Make a Deal - To negotiate a new way of dividing the money among the top finishers at the last table in a tournament.

Make a Move - To try to bluff. "When the board paired sixes, Max *made a move* at the pot. I thought that he was bluffing but I had nothing to call him with."

Middle Buster - An inside straight draw. "If the flop comes A-10-4 and you have the Q-J, you're not going to draw to the *middle buster* to try to catch the king."

(The) Nut Draw - You have a draw to the best possible hand. "When two clubs come on the board and you have the A♣ J♣, you have the *nut* flush *draw*."

(The) Nuts - The best hand possible in any given pot. "Remember that you can flop the *nuts* and lose it on the turn; for example, when you flop the nut straight and the board pairs making a full house for your opponent."

Nutted Up - When someone is playing very tight. "Jackson was so *nutted up* at the final table, I stole pot after pot from him."

(An) Out - A card that completes your hand. "Always try to have an extra *out*, a third low card to go with your ace, when you're drawing for the low end."

Overpair - A pair in your hand made up of cards higher than the highest card showing on the board. "When the board came Q-J-6, I had an *overpair* with my pocket kings."

Pay Off - To call an opponent's bet at the river even though you think that he might have the best hand. "When the board paired at the river, I decided to *pay him off* when he bet because I wasn't sure that he had made trips."

Payout - The prize money you win at the end of the tournament.

Peddling the Nuts - Drawing to, playing, and betting the nut hand. "Players may not always be peddling the nuts in a heads-up situation, but in any multiway pot somebody's usually drawing at the nuts if he doesn't already have it."

Piece Yourself Out - To raise your tournament buy-in by selling shares of your potential winnings. "I had *pieced myself out* three ways, so I didn't have a huge payday."

Play Back - Responding to an opponent's bet by either raising or reraising. "If a tight opponent *plays back* at you, you know he probably has the nuts."

Play From Behind - Checking with the intent of check-raising when you have a big hand. "I knew that Kevin usually *played from behind* when he had a big hand so when he checked, so did I."

Play Fast - Aggressively betting a drawing hand to get full value for it if you make it. "Many players *play fast* in the early rounds of rebuy tournaments to try to build their stacks."

Play Slow - The opposite of playing fast. To wait and see what develops before pushing a hand. "When you make the nut straight on the flop and there's a chance that the flush draw is out or possibly a set, why not play your hand *slow* to start with?" (The opposite of "playing fast.")

Play With - Staying in the hand by betting calling, raising, or reraising. "You should realize that you're going to *get played with* most of the time because hold'em is a limit-structure game."

Put on the Heat - To pressure your opponents with aggressive betting strategies to get the most value from your hand. "You might consider *putting on the heat* when your opponent is slightly conservative or when he has a short stack against your big stack."

Put Them on (a Hand) - To assign a certain value to an opponent's hand. "Using my instincts and how he played the hand, I *put Stanley on* the nut low."

Rag (or Blank) - A board card that doesn't help appears not to have helped anyone at the table. "The flop came with A-2-3 and then a *rag*, the 9♠, hit on the turn."

Rag Off - The river card doesn't help you. "Then it *ragged off* on the end and he was a gone goose for all his money."

Rainbow Flop - The flop cards are three different suits. "I liked my straight draw when the flop came *rainbow* and nobody could have a flush draw against me."

Read the Board - To understand the value of your hand in relation to the cards on the board. "If you *read the board* correctly, you often can tell where you're at in the hand by the action."

Rebuy Event - If you go broke early in the tournament, you can buy more chips (usually during the first three rounds only). "I made three $500 rebuys in the $500 pot-limit Omaha *rebuy event*."

Round - The predetermined length of time that each betting increment is in force during a tournament (20 minutes, one hour, and so on).

Run Over - To play aggressively in an attempt to control the other players. "If they're not trying to stop you from being a bully, then keep *running over them* until they do."

Runner-Runner - To catch cards on the turn and river that make your hand a winner. "As it turns out, you had a suited K-J, caught *runner-runner* to make a flush, and broke me!"

Second-Hand Low – To limp-in behind a raiser on the pre-flop, usually with aces, hoping that a player behind reraises, so that you can come over the top of him.

Showdown - When no one bets at the river and the cards are turned over to determine the winner. "If everyone checks to you at the river and you couldn't win in a *showdown*, why bet if you know that you will get called?"

Shut Down - To stop playing aggressively. "When the board paired the second highest card, I decided to *shut down*."

Slowplay - To refrain from betting a strong hand for maximum value because you are hoping to trap your opponents. "I knew the rock in the third seat was *slowplaying* aces so I didn't bet my set when he checked on the flop."

Smooth Call - To call a bet without raising. "If someone bets into you, you might *smooth call* with this type of hand because you have an extra out."

Solid Player - An accomplished player who employs the right strategy at all times. "I decided not to call Boston's raise because I knew he was a *solid player* who wouldn't get out of line."

Stand a Raise - To call a raise. "I recently *stood a raise* in a cash game with 9-8 on the button. The board came 7-6-2, no suits. A guy led off with a decent bet and I called him with my overcards and a straight draw."

Stiffed In - To play a blind hand in an unraised pot. "The only time that you might play 7-2 in hold'em is when you are *stiffed in* in the big blind."

Surrender - To give up on your hand. "When the fourth flush card hit at the river, I had to *surrender*."

Survival Tactics - To play conservatively rather than bet for maximum value in an attempt to last longer in the tournament.

Take off a Card - To call a bet on the flop. "I decided to *take off a card* and see what the turn would bring."

Takeoff Hand - A hand that has the potential to beat a better starting hand because it's live. "In four-way action, I figured that my middle connectors might turn into a *takeoff hand*."

Take Them Off (a hand) - To beat a superior starting hand. "Any of those types of hands in which you have two straight cards and a pair will *take the aces right off* a lot of times."

Tell - A mannerism that a player exhibits at the table that tips off an opponent to what he's holding or how he's likely to play the hand.

Underpair - A pair that is lower than a pair showing on the board. "Why would you ever want to call with an *underpair*?"

Wake Up With a Hand - You are dealt a hand with winning potential. "Just because a player is a maniac doesn't mean that he can't *wake up with a hand*. Over the long haul, everybody gets the same number of good hands and bad hands."

Weak Ace - You have an ace in your hand but you do not have a high kicker to go with it. "I won't bet a *weak ace* unless I am certain that I have the only ace at the table."

Where You're At - You understand the value of your hand in relation to the other players' hands. "Your opponent may not know for sure where you're at in the hand when you have played it in a deceptive way."

FROM CARDOZA'S EXCITING LIBRARY
ADD THESE TO YOUR COLLECTION - ORDER NOW!

POKER WISDOM OF A CHAMPION by Doyle Brunson. Learn what it takes to be a great poker player by climbing inside the mind of poker's most famous champion. Fascinating anecdotes and adventures from Doyle's early career playing poker in roadhouses and with other great champions are interspersed with important lessons you can learn from the man who has made more money at poker than anyone else in the history of the game. You'll learn what makes a great player tick, how he approaches the game, and receive candid, powerful advice from the legend himself. The Mad Genius of poker, Mike Caro, says, "Brunson is the greatest poker player who ever lived. This book shows why." 192 pages. $14.95.

CARO'S BOOK OF POKER TELLS by Mike Caro. The classic book is now revised and back in print! This long-awaited brand new edition by the Mad Genius of Poker takes a detailed look at the art and science of tells, the physical giveaways by players on their hands. Featuring photos of poker players in action along with Caro's explanations about when players are bluffing and when they're not. These powerful eye-opening ideas can give you the decisive edge at the table! This invaluable book should be in every player's library! 320 pages. $24.95.

KEN WARREN TEACHES TEXAS HOLD'EM by Ken Warren. This is a step-by-step comprehensive manual for making money at hold'em poker. 42 powerful chapters will teach you one lesson at a time. Great practical advice and concepts with examples from actual games and how to apply them to your own play. Lessons include: Starting Cards, Playing Position, Which Hands to Play, Raising, Check-raising, Tells, Game/Seat Selection, Dominated Hands, Odds, and much more. This book is already a huge fan favorite and best-seller! 416 pages. $26.95.

WINNERS GUIDE TO TEXAS HOLD'EM POKER by Ken Warren. The most powerful book on beating hold'em shows serious players how to play every hand from every position with every type of flop. Learn the 14 categories of starting hands, the 10 most common hold'em tells, how to evaluate a game for profit, value of deception, art of bluffing, eight secrets to winning, starting hand categories, position, and more! Bonus: Includes detailed analysis of the top 40 hands and the most complete chapter on hold'em odds in print. Over 500,000 copies in print. 224 pages. $16.95.

THE BIG BOOK OF POKER by Ken Warren. This easy-to-read and oversized guide teaches you everything you need to know to win money at home poker, in cardrooms, casinos and on the tournament circuit. Readers will learn how to bet, raise, and checkraise, bluff, semi-bluff, and how to take advantage of position and pot odds. Great sections on hold'em (plus, stud games, Omaha, draw games, and many more) and playing and winning poker on the internet. Packed with charts, diagrams, sidebars, and detailed, easy-to-read examples by best-selling poker expert Ken Warren, this wonderfully formatted book is one stop shopping for players ready to take on any form of poker for real money. Want to be a big player? Buy the *Big Book of Poker*! 320 oversized pages. $19.95.

HOW TO PLAY WINNING POKER by Avery Cardoza. New and expanded edition shows playing and winning strategies for all major games: 5 and 7-stud games, Omaha, draw poker, hold'em, and high-low, both for home and casino play. You'll learn 15 winning poker concepts, how to minimize losses and maximize profits, how to read opponents and gain the edge against their style, how to use pot odds, tells, position, more. 160 pages. $12.95.

THE CHAMPIONSHIP SERIES
POWERFUL BOOKS YOU MUST HAVE

CHAMPIONSHIP HOLD'EM by Tom McEvoy & T.J. Cloutier. Hard-hitting hold'em the way it's played today in both limit cash games and tournaments. Get killer advice on how to win more money in rammin'-jammin' games, kill-pot, jackpot, shorthanded, and other types of cash games. You'll learn the thinking process before the flop, on the flop, on the turn, and at the river with specific suggestions for what to do when good or bad things happen plus 20 illustrated hands with play-by-play analyses. Specific advice for rocks in tight games, weaklings in loose games, experts in solid games, how hand values change in jackpot games, when you should fold, check, raise, reraise, check-raise, slowplay, bluff, and tournament strategies for small buy-in, big buy-in, rebuy, incremental add-on, satellite and big-field major tournaments. Wow! Easy-to-read and conversational, if you want to become a lifelong winner at limit hold'em, you need this book! 388 Pages, Illustrated, Photos. $39.95. Now only $29.95!

CHAMPIONSHIP NO-LIMIT & POT-LIMIT HOLD'EM by T.J. Cloutier & Tom McEvoy. New Cardoza Edition! The definitive guide to winning at two of the world's most exciting poker games! Written by eight time World Champion players T.J. Cloutier (1998 and 2002 Player of the Year) and Tom McEvoy (the foremost author on tournament strategy) who have won millions of dollars each playing no-limit and pot-limit hold'em in cash games and major tournaments around the world. You'll get all the answers here—no holds barred—to your most important questions: How do you get inside your opponents' heads and learn how to beat them at their own game? How can you tell how much to bet, raise, and reraise in no-limit hold'em? When can you bluff? How do you set up your opponents in pot-limit hold'em so you can win a monster pot? What are the best strategies for winning no-limit and pot-limit tournaments, satellites, and supersatellites? You get rock-solid and inspired advice from two of the most recognizable figures in poker—advice that you can bank on. If you want to become a winning player, and a champion, you must have this book. 304 pages, paperback, illustrations, photos. $29.95

CHAMPIONSHIP OMAHA (Omaha High-Low, Pot-limit Omaha, Limit High Omaha) by Tom McEvoy & T.J. Cloutier. Clearly-written strategies and powerful advice from Cloutier and McEvoy who have won four World Series of Poker titles in Omaha tournaments. Powerful advice shows you how to win at low-limit and high-stakes games, how to play against loose and tight opponents, and the differing strategies for rebuy and freezeout tournaments. Learn the best starting hands, when slowplaying a big hand is dangerous, what danglers are and why winners don't play them, why pot-limit Omaha is the only poker game where you sometimes fold the nuts on the flop and are correct in doing so and overall, and how you can win a lot of money at Omaha! 230 pages, photos, illustrations, $39.95. Now only $29.95!

CHAMPIONSHIP STUD (Seven-Card Stud, Stud 8/or Better and Razz) by Dr. Max Stern, Linda Johnson, and Tom McEvoy. The authors, who have earned millions of dollars in major tournaments and cash games, eight World Series of Poker bracelets and hundreds of other titles in competition against the best players in the world show you the winning strategies for medium-limit side games as well as poker tournaments and a general tournament strategy that is applicable to any form of poker. Includes give-and-take conversations between the authors to give you more than one point of view on how to play poker. 200 pages, hand pictorials, photos. $39.95.

THE CHAMPIONSHIP SERIES
POWERFUL BOOKS YOU MUST HAVE

CHAMPIONSHIP TOURNAMENT POKER by Tom McEvoy. New Cardoza Edition! Rated by pros as best book on tournaments ever written and enthusiastically endorsed by more than five world champions, this is the definitive guide to winning tournaments and a must for every player's library. McEvoy lets you in on the secrets he has used to win millions of dollars in tournaments and the insights he has learned competing against the best players in the world. Packed solid with winning strategies for all 11 games in the World Series of Poker, with extensive discussions of 7-card stud, limit hold'em, pot and no-limit hold'em, Omaha high-low, re-buy, half-half tournaments, satellites, and strategies for each stage of tournaments. Tons of essential concepts and specific strategies jam-pack the book. Phil Hellmuth, 1989 WSOP champion says, "[this] is the world's most definitive guide to winning poker tournaments." 416 pages, paperback, $29.95.

CHAMPIONSHIP TABLE (at the World Series of Poker) by Dana Smith, Ralph Wheeler, and Tom McEvoy. New Cardoza Edition! From 1970 when the champion was presented a silver cup, to the present when the champion was awarded more than $2 million, *Championship Table* celebrates three decades of poker greats who have competed to win poker's most coveted title. This book gives you the names and photographs of all the players who made the final table, pictures of the last hand the champion played against the runner-up, how they played their cards, and how much they won. This book also features fascinating interviews and conversations with the champions and runners-up and interesting highlights from each Series. This is a fascinating and invaluable resource book for WSOP and gaming buffs. In some cases the champion himself wrote "how it happened," as did two-time champion Doyle Brunson when Stu Ungar caught a wheel in 1980 on the turn to deprive "Texas Dolly" of his third title. Includes tons of vintage photographs. 208 pages, paperback, $19.95.

CHAMPIONSHIP SATELLITE STRATEGY by Brad Daugherty & Tom McEvoy. In 2002 and 2003, satellite players won their way into the $10,000 WSOP buy-in and emerged as champions, winning more than $2 million each. You can too! You'll learn specific, proven strategies for winning almost any satellite. Learn the ten ways to win a seat at the WSOP and other big tournaments, how to win limit hold'em and no-limit hold'em satellites, one-table satellites for big tournaments, and online satellites, plus how to play the final table of super satellites. McEvoy and Daugherty sincerely believe that if you practice these strategies, you can win your way into any tournament for a fraction of the buy-in. You'll learn how much to bet, how hard to pressure opponents, how to tell when an opponent is bluffing, how to play deceptively, and how to use your chips as weapons of destruction. Includes a special chapter on no-limit hold'em satellites! 256 pages. Illustrated hands, photos, glossary. $24.95.

CHAMPIONSHIP HOLD'EM TOURNAMENT HANDS by T.J. Cloutier & Tom McEvoy. Two tournament legends show you how to become a winning tournament player. Get inside their heads as they think their way through the correct strategy at 57 limit and no-limit practice hands. Cloutier and McEvoy show you how to use your skill and intuition to play strategic hands for maximum profit in real tournament scenarios and how 45 key hands were played by champions in turnaround situations at the WSOP. By sharing their analysis on how the winners and losers played key hands, you'll gain tremendous insights into how tournament poker is played at the highest levels. Learn how champions think and how they play major hands in strategic tournament situations, Cloutier and McEvoy believe that you will be able to win your share of the profits in today's tournaments—and join them at the championship table far sooner than you ever imagined. 368 pages, illustrated with card pictures, $29.95

POWERFUL POKER SIMULATIONS
A MUST FOR SERIOUS PLAYERS WITH A COMPUTER!
IBM compatibles CD ROM Win 95, 98, 2000, NT, ME, XP - Full Color Graphics

These **incredible** full color poker simulation programs are the absolute **best** method to improve your game. Computer opponents play like real players. All games let you set the limits and rake, have fully programmable players, adjustable lineup, stat tracking, and Hand Analyzer for starting hands. Mike Caro, the world's foremost poker theoretician says, "Amazing..a steal for under $500..get it, it's great." Includes free telephone support. "Smart Advisor" gives expert advice for every play in every game!

1. TURBO TEXAS HOLD'EM FOR WINDOWS - $89.95 - Choose which players, how many, 2-10, you want to play, create loose/tight game, control check-raising, bluffing, position, sensitivity to pot odds, more! Also, instant replay, pop-up odds, Professional Advisor, keeps track of play statistics. Free bonus: Hold'em Hand Analyzer analyzes all 169 pocket hands in detail, their win rates under any conditions you set. Caro says this "hold'em software is the most powerful ever created." Great product!

2. TURBO SEVEN-CARD STUD FOR WINDOWS - $89.95 - Create any conditions of play; choose number of players (2-8), bet amounts, fixed or spread limit, bring-in method, tight/loose conditions, position, reaction to board, number of dead cards, stack deck to create special conditions, instant replay. Terrific stat reporting includes analysis of starting cards, 3-D bar charts, graphs. Play interactively, run high speed simulation to test strategies. Hand Analyzer analyzes starting hands in detail. Wow!

3. TURBO OMAHA HIGH-LOW SPLIT FOR WINDOWS - $89.95 -Specify any playing conditions; betting limits, number of raises, blind structures, button position, aggressiveness/passiveness of opponents, number of players (2-10), types of hands dealt, blinds, position, board reaction, specify flop, turn, river cards! Choose opponents, use provided point count or create your own. Statistical reporting, instant replay, pop-up odds, high speed simulation to test strategies, amazing Hand Analyzer, much more!

4. TURBO OMAHA HIGH FOR WINDOWS - $89.95 - Same features as above, but tailored for Omaha High-only. Caro says program is "an electrifying research tool..it can clearly be worth thousands of dollars to any serious player. A must for Omaha High players.

5. TURBO 7 STUD 8 OR BETTER - $89.95 - Brand new with all the features you expect from the Wilson Turbo products: the latest artificial intelligence, instant advice and exact odds, play versus 2-7 opponents, enhanced data charts that can be exported or printed, the ability to fold out of turn and immediately go to the next hand, ability to peek at opponents hand, optional warning mode that warns you if a play disagrees with the advisor, and automatic testing mode that can run up to 50 tests unattended. Challenge tough computer players who vary their styles for a truly great poker game.

6. TOURNAMENT TEXAS HOLD'EM - $59.95

Set-up for tournament practice and play, this realistic simulation pits you against celebrity look-alikes. Tons of options let you control tournament size with 10 to 300 entrants, select limits, ante, rake, blind structures, freezeouts, number of rebuys and competition level of opponents - average, tough, or toughest. Pop-up status report shows how you're doing vs. the competition. Save tournaments in progress to play again later. Additional feature allows you to quickly finish a folded hand and go on to the next.